Power Tools©

Build People
Who Succeed in Life and
You Build Business that
Succeeds for Life

by Walter P. Spires, Jr.

KENDALL/HUNT PUBLISHING COMPANY
4050 Westmark Drive   Dubuque, Iowa 52002

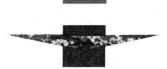

Table of Contents

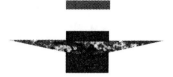

Acknowledgments

The process of creating a book is just that . . . a process. It involves a great deal more than transcribing the author's writing and binding the pages. The process usually involves a number of people, and this one is no exception.

I chose a somewhat unique method of acknowledging many (certainly not all) of the people who have impacted or influenced my life through relationships, and thus indirectly influenced the writing of this book. I have written a tribute of sorts to these people, and you will find it in the Appendix of this book. I recognize that many readers skip the "stuff" in the front and back of books. While I am told that tributes like these basically serve my purposes and contribute little to the book content, that's okay. I really wanted to esteem these people and communicate how much I value/valued the relationships over the years.

Back to this book specifically. I want to thank Hal Hawkins, Associate Managing Editor, of Kendall/Hunt for his editing input, advice and, most of all, his encouragement regarding the usefulness of the content throughout this process. I also want to thank the team at Kendall/Hunt who helped with all the other "stuff" like cover design and other valuable input that made the manuscript a book.

I would also like to thank Duncan Jaenicke for his input early in the process as I worked to sort out my thoughts. In this same vein, my good friend, Charles Boyd also gave me some valuable input in the formative stages.

Without a doubt, though, this book would not have happened without the help and support of the person whose relationship I value so greatly, my wife, lover, and friend, Gigi. Her diligence in wading through rough drafts, listening and responding to me "thinking out loud," and giving me the freedom to work the hours necessary to complete such an enormous undertaking were nothing short of wonderful. While my children are young and may not totally understand what this is all about, I want to thank Trey and Gracie for their support and interest as I wrote, and little Zach for simply being a significant part of our family. I really treasure you three!

Finally, I want to thank those of you who are about to read this book. I hope you will *apply* these tools in your personal and professional lives. I pray they will make a significant difference.

PART ONE

Forming Tools—
The Focus is Me

INTRODUCTION

Corporate down-sizing, "do more with less," re-engineering, and picking up the pieces of what is left behind. World-class customer service and delighting our customers. Total quality, continuous improvement, employee involvement and empowerment initiatives. What do they all have in common? PEOPLE. People interacting with other people . . . **relationships**.

Consider the "customer from hell" who gives you the business, and then really "gives you the business!" They demand world-class service, nickel and dime you to death on price, and then drag out payables for 120 days! Don't you love 'em? NO! Be honest. You want to call them names. For Christmas you want to send them a one way ticket for a vacation in Iraq! BUT you don't do any of these things (unless you have another job lined up).

Let's face it, folks. Unless you live on the moon (or in Big Sky country), all your life you are going to face or deal with imperfect beings we call . . . **people**. You're going to have to work with, buy from, sell to, live with or next door to *people*. Your business and personal success are often, to a large extent, in the hands of *other people*.

From the jerk in front of you driving too slow to the idiot who nearly blew your doors off driving too fast, they are there. From the high control manager who insists on signing off on purchase requisitions for paper clips and coffee filters to the non-confrontational manager who does your annual performance review by voice-mail, we're stuck with them.

Unless you are a genius or lucky enough to invent something that brings you wealth and fame (like a pill that grows hair or concoction that dissolves fat cells) *or* unless you "marry well," about the only way to really succeed in life is by building successful relationships with people. This book is intended for people who fall into one of three categories. Those who *buy-in*, those who *give-in* or those who *cave-in*.

The first group (buy-in) are probably already doing well in most of their personal and professional relationships. They take the TQM (total quality management) approach to relationships and want to continuously improve that which is already pretty good.

The second group (give-in) will buy this book and put it on the shelf to make their library at the office or home look better. OR they will put it on their bookshelf to make other people *think* they are concerned about people and relationships. But they can't fool us. Occasionally, they will open it up, skim the table of contents, and flip through the pages. Then it happens.

They read something that grabs their attention. Perhaps it is something they disagree with so they read on to see if anyone could really be as opinionated as this "stuff" sounds to them. But by the time they finish, they begin to think, perhaps, I am not so dumb after all. Maybe there is some truth to what I have to say. So they finish reading it and commit to work on the action plan points to build successful people.

The third group (cave-in) wouldn't buy this book on a bet. If they have the book at all, it was *given* to them as a present! These are the people (husbands, wives, co-workers, etc.) who others wish would read it. They typically have huge *blind spots* when it comes to relationships. They think they are doing great. They tend to suffer from that "legend in their own mind" syndrome. We all know them. How do we help them *see the blindspots*?

Perhaps you can chip in and buy them this book as a present and not put your names on the card. Sign it "from those who care." Or if they are really bad, you could do the old *deodorant trick*. Leave a copy of the book on their desk along with a can of deodorant. Write on the card "when it comes to relationships with people . . . you really stink it up!" Maybe not. After all we are trying to help encourage and empower other people; particularly those who need it the most. If these people ever really "get it," it is because things get so bad, or they get so desperate, they finally *cave-in*.

So I wrote this book for those people who (regardless of how they get here) see the value of *building people who succeed in life*, starting with themselves. You may be struggling personally with issues ranging from character, to getting along with people, to what you want to be when you really *grow up*.

At home, you may be struggling to re-gain balance in your personal life. You feel the need to build (or re-build) those vital relationships with your family. At work, you *can't do any more with any less*, even if that is the *corporate mantra*. You want to really understand how you can work smarter because you can't work any harder.

If any of these scenarios fit, then the contents of this book should help. I consider the book a TOOLBOX of sorts. A toolbox of *Power Tools* to equip you to build people and relationships that succeed in life.

Even before I began the actual writing, I thought of the analogy of the power tools and toolbox. My dad and I had been building a play center for the kids in the backyard. The project grew tremendously from when I first sketched it out in my mind. It went from being a one story play fort to a two story one. Then I added a fireman's pole to slide down. Next a "secret escape" hatch and a zip line to fly down to the ground. How would I ever accomplish the task?

The answer lay in two things. The first was getting help from other people. In this case, it was my dad. My dad is incredibly talented when it comes to building things. And when it comes to projects for his grandkids, his energy seems endless. (Thanks dad, for lending your experience, a strong back, and a helping hand.)

The second part of the answer was using the right *power tools*. They were a tremendous resource to have available. They made the job easier and reduced the time it took to complete it. I believe the *power tools* in this book can do the same for you.

Building from the Ground Up
. . . The Issue is Character

"Character is what you are in the dark."

D. L. MOODY

ow do you define character? The dictionary defines it as *the combination of qualities and attributes that distinguishes an individual.* The quotation above is probably the best working definition I've read. A paraphrase could read *who you are and what you do when no one else is around.*

Abraham Lincoln described it as follows. "Character is like a tree and reputation like its shadow. The shadow is what we think of it; the tree is the real thing." One of Solomon's proverbs says "As a man thinks in his heart, so is he." Character is the foundation upon which you build the rest of your life. It comes into play in all aspects of our lives: personal, professional, and social. Whether you are alone with a crucial personal decision or in an executive meeting deciding how to cut 15,000 jobs, your true character will surface and show itself.

Allow me to share with you a couple of very old stories that demonstrate outstanding character displayed in the face of extreme difficulty and adversity. The first concerns four young Jewish men who demonstrated outstanding character under the threat of hardship, persecution and even death. Their names were Hananiah, Mishael, Azariah and Daniel. If you are familiar with Old Testament bible stories, you know the first three better as Shadrach, Meshach and

7

Abednigo. These four youths were taken captive when the Baby-
lonians conquered the nation of Israel circa 600 B.C.

Funny thing about these four. They were observed to be different;
special in some way. They were chosen to be part of the king's *management development program* even though they were captive foreign-
ers. They were above all else young men of character.

Part of the king's program regimen included a diet containing
foods that Daniel and his friends' religion did not permit them to
eat. To do so would violate principles by which these four lived. So
Daniel, being sort of the spokesperson, went to his manager and
asked permission not to eat the king's food. This put his manager
in a tough spot. He knew that if he permitted this and the four
young men got sick or looked worse than the others in the program,
he would not only lose his job, but his life!

Daniel suggested a *pilot program.* "Give us ten days," he said, "on
fresh vegetables and water, and see how we do." Their manager
agreed, and at the end of the ten days they looked great! They did
so well that they looked (and were) healthier than all the rest, so
their manager permitted them to remain with this diet. In time, they
were promoted into the king's personal service. This seemingly mild
challenge was only a shadow of later tests to come.

Later under another king, these same four men faced much greater
tests of character. In the first situation, Daniel, now third in com-
mand in the entire country was politically set up by those jealous
of his position. These men observed that Daniel prayed regularly
three times a day. So they tricked the king into signing a law that
prohibited seeking help (including praying) from anyone but the
king for thirty days. This violated "core values" of Daniel, and he
continued his habit of praying three times a day (as his enemies
knew he would.)

Well, as you might guess, Daniel was *caught* and sentenced to
death in the lion's den. Raw meat, so to speak. Most of us know the
story had a happy ending with God delivering Daniel in a miracu-
lous way. His uncompromising character and personal faith were
demonstrated throughout the process.

What happened to the other three? Later we find Shadrach, Meshach and Abednigo standing before a different king, only this time *they* were in big trouble. It seems this king (a man of questionable character himself) created an idol of gold before which everyone was supposed to bow. Since this was a clear violation of one of their governing principles, they refused to obey.

Because the king had always liked these three, he gave them another chance and a choice to make. Bow down before the gold statue or be thrown into a furnace of fire to burn to death. These men of character chose death over violating their personal beliefs and principles. As it did with Daniel, this story ended happily as the three were delivered from a fiery death.

However, we know from history and more recent experience that this is not always the case. Many men and women of great character have suffered greatly and even forfeited their lives for causes they deemed worthy or to defend principles they held in high esteem.

Another more recent story (unfortunately) demonstrates *lack* of character. This was seen through the vandalism and looting in the aftermath of the Los Angeles earthquake. People were seen on camera stealing from neighbors and business owners in their own communities and neighborhoods. In these pathetic scenes, people took advantage of circumstances in which authority or control couldn't be exercised, and their real character (or lack of it) surfaced.

When you think of people of character, who comes to mind? Many of us think of the early leaders in our own nation's history. We think of those women and men who lead worthy causes and movements, and those who served their country well during wars and other hardships. When the polls are taken for the most respected and admired people in the world, two people have consistently remained on the list, not for years but decades. They are Mother Teresa and Dr. Billy Graham.

Why is it that they continue to head the lists of most respected people in the world? Is it because they are *religious* people? Not necessarily, because many of those surveyed are not religious people. Is it because they seek it out in campaigning? No, quite the opposite is true. The answer lies in their character. They embody those qualities of impeccable character in what they believe, say and do. Their consistency of outstanding character extends over a lifetime, not just an isolated event or act, but a *lifetime*.

"Okay," you say, "you've given us examples of characters from thousands of years ago and current *religious* leaders, BUT how can I relate this to me today, where I am? And what about applying it to the workplace?" The balance of this chapter addresses just that. But before we move on, I think it only fair to give credit where credit is due.

All of us come up with thoughts and ideas "on our own" usually after reading something someone else has written. I often tell my audiences that Solomon said it best, "There is nothing new under the sun." That doesn't mean there aren't new or different perspectives, but I've yet to see much truly "new" in the areas of leadership, empowerment and high performance work groups (those subjects on which I speak, write and consult).

To that end, in addition to the reference resource I used for the stories (the Bible), authors Stephen Covey (*Seven Habits of Highly Effective People*) and Robert Clinton (*Making of a Leader*) have provided valuable insights and perspectives on the issue of character. So just as you would do if you were writing this, you sieve what others have said through your own paradigms, combine it with personal perspectives and experience, and hope what falls out offers additional insights on the subject.

The primary purpose of this chapter is to help you understand what goes into making up a person's character, and to see that outstanding personal character is the foundation upon which we build success in our personal and professional lives. Hopefully examining your own character and assessing your own character attributes will provide you with a personal development plan and help you work toward *raising the (character) bar*.

TWO SIDES OF CHARACTER

What is meant by saying there are *two sides to a person's character?* I
believe they are best described as the *being* side and a *doing* side. Simply stated, *we are* and then *we do.* Let's consider first the *being* side.

The *Being* Side

The being side of a person's character is what Moody refers to in the
"what we are in the dark" quote. When there is no one else around
and you have some time to reflect from an *internal* perspective, what
do you see? Do you like what you see? Some of us may relate to Ava
Gardner's comical statement, "Deep down, I'm really superficial."
Unfortunately today there are too many who not only relate to this,
but are very superficial . . . "a mile wide and an inch deep."

Personal selfishness consumes them. They often sit around with
their favorite possession, their mirror, to see how they look to the
world.

*People of outstanding character replace their mirrors with
windows so they can look out into the real world and see
how they might be useful and help others.*

Developing outstanding personal character is accomplished first
by understanding who you are, deciding where you want to be, and
then developing a plan to "deepen the roots."

One of the more empowering thoughts concerning the being side
of character is that *you control it.* There aren't many things in life
that we can control as individuals, but character is one. I choose to
be who I am, and I choose who I will be. Few would argue that
character traits, like values, are strongly influenced by people and
the environment in which they are raised. However, we also know
that people of outstanding character rise above negative people
and circumstances **to be**come responsible contributors to our society. They learn and grow from their experiences.

The *Doing* Side

This is where the "rubber meets the road," "your walk talks," "actions speak louder than words" (and all the other behavior-related clichés). The doing side is just that . . . what you do. Your actions and behaviors tell the real tale of your character. Three things are revealed from the doing side of our character.

The first is *personal congruence*. (By the way, congruence means harmony or agreement.) Personal congruence has to do with congruence between who you know you really are, and what you do. It may seem too visceral (warm and fuzzy) for some of you, but it is real and important. I call it the *peace* factor. Do I have peace of mind that my attitudes and actions are congruent or *in synch?*

For example, when I try to be something I am not, the peace factor drops considerably, and I know it. Consider a very aggressive, demanding manager. We'll call him Mr. Jerk. He doesn't value the people for whom he has responsibility and tends to look in his *mirror* a lot. He is mostly concerned about his own personal success, typically at the expense of others. Suppose Mr. Jerk goes through one of our empowerment programs. (By the way, he attends only because he has to.) He has no interest in changing and decides this empowerment stuff is the latest *flavor of the month.*

He has a small problem because his boss has become a convert to the principles of empowerment and wants to see everyone manage their staffs accordingly. Mr. Jerk is stuck. He may be a jerk, but he is no dummy. He knows that keeping his job means at least going through the motions. Here is where it happens. His internal peace level goes way down, and his stress level goes way up. When we act (by force or otherwise) *out of character*, the result is *stress*. Mr. Jerk now will actually make everyone else more miserable (including himself) by acting out of character because of the second factor—*credibility*. He doesn't have any.

Credibility is defined as *the power to elicit belief*. Whether or not I have this power is based on other people's feelings about whether or not my *talk* and *walk* are in alignment. Most of us have personally experienced this when we were teenagers. It had to do with our attitudes toward our parents. As teens, we were simply trying to *get a life* (to put it in today's jargon).

Part of the process involved watching adults, especially our parents, to see if they really believed all the *stuff* they had been pouring into our heads. We wanted to see them living it out. It is during this stage that many teens learn the word *hypocrite* and use it more than we like. Credibility comes from character; the *doing* side of character. It is earned from the third factor—*consistency*.

Whether it is your teenage son or daughter, or the people with whom you work, everyone bases character judgments to a great extent on your *consistency*. Two good words that describe it are *reliability* and *uniformity*. It is staying the course for the long haul. It means not bailing out when things get tough or societal norms change around you (even if it means being *politically incorrect*).

Consistency of character endures. If this isn't true, then why is it that throughout the course of history with the billions of people who have lived or are living, we tend to remember only those whose characters stand out, either extremely positive or negative.

Following is a list of attributes of people who possess positively outstanding character. It is for your personal consideration and evaluation. It is not meant to be exhaustive, but does embody the key tools for building outstanding character.

RESPECT

This implies respect for *self* and *others*. It means to value and esteem people, their rights and property. We value the dignity and sanctity of human life. We value people as our most valuable natural resource. AND we respect the differences that exist among ourselves. It begins with self-respect. People who have little self-respect usually demonstrate little, if any, respect for others. This subject will be discussed in more detail in Chapter 8. Suffice it to say that without respect, not even the shallowest of relationships can exist.

INTEGRITY

The word integrity comes from the Latin word *integritas*, and is where we get our word integer. You may recall that *integer* means whole or undivided. People of integrity are whole or undivided themselves. Another definition is *steadfast adherence to a strict moral or ethical code*. I like to describe it as *beliefs in action* and *congruence between beliefs and behaviors*.

Integrity is not something held inside a person. It is not an internal quality. Rather it is an external one that is demonstrated to others through our actions. While it is by nature silent, it speaks volumes about our character. Finally, a person of integrity *does not compromise* her beliefs in difficult times or for the sake of expediency or for self-promotion.

HONESTY

Surely honesty is not the best policy? If it were there wouldn't be as many wars and political conflicts. There wouldn't be as much crime. There wouldn't be as many lawsuits. Would there? This may be the most basic quality of these listed here, but it has become, for some, a difficult one to live out. This isn't *rocket science*, folks.

The dictionary defines honesty as *principled uprightness of character and adherence to a strict moral or ethical code*. We understand that, don't we? In layman's terms it means *tell the truth, treat people fairly, and obey the laws and principles that govern you*.

Begin with yourself. Be honest with yourself about yourself. If you can't do that, you certainly can't do it with other people. Remember, too, that honesty is not a situationally dependent issue. Principles based in truth never are.

Two things open the door for potential trouble. The first is when we start rationalizing "our unique situation" to justify bending the rules. The second and most dangerous is the *theory of relativity*. Not Einstein's. This one is my *character-related* version. It is when one person considers his own behavior relative to someone else's and judges that it is OK because what he *will do, is doing,* or *has done* certainly isn't as bad (relatively speaking of course) as someone else's behavior. This *theory of relativity* tends to rule out moral absolutes which leads us to the next quality of outstanding character.

MORAL ABSOLUTES

The dictionary defines morality as *conduct in accordance with principles and standards; a system of right and wrong conduct.* It is interesting to note that phrases very similar to these are used with the words *integrity* and *honesty* in the text of the dictionary below the synonym definitions for each word.

You may be wondering why I keep giving you dictionary definitions for these words. There is a purpose. It is to avoid having you think that I am simply passing along personal opinions based primarily on personal values. Rather, I hope you are seeing that these qualities are tied together. I also hope you believe, as most people do, that they only hold together when anchored or moored to some absolute guiding truths and principles. I know that the deeper we go into this subject, the more likely someone will get upset and say this is really a values issue (which we will discuss in Chapter 4). It isn't.

To substantiate this I suggest you simply study the history of civilization and see what happens when people are guided by or live in principle-less, value-less societies. To save you some time, the answer is—they don't survive. It usually goes something like this: moral decline, political chaos, anarchy, and finally, captivity or extinction.

RESPONSIBILITY

People of outstanding character are responsible people. You can count on them to do what they said they would do. They are dependable. They accept personal responsibility for their *attitudes* and *actions*. They act responsibly toward others.

COURAGE

People of outstanding character demonstrate courage. They may find themselves in situations where they face personal danger (as noted in the stories shared earlier). They may also find themselves in other situations where the expedient solution is to simply compromise. But courageous people of outstanding character don't compromise where it counts.

The courageous person stands in the gap to help others in need. He doesn't just go along with the crowd when he knows it isn't the right thing to do. The courageous person of outstanding character doesn't have to wear medals or sound his own horn. Rather he is surprised when people make a big *to-do* over someone doing something that comes naturally.

I want to close this chapter with a story I have read to my children many times. It is from *The Velveteen Rabbit*, a children's storybook classic. The dialog takes place in a little boy's nursery between two primary characters who happen to be stuffed animals, the Skin Horse and the Velveteen Rabbit.

> *"What is real?" asked the rabbit one day, when they were lying side by side near the nursery fender, before Nana came to tidy the room. "Does it mean having things that buzz inside you and a stick-out handle?"*
>
> *"Real isn't how you are made," said the Skin Horse. "It's a thing that happens to you. When a child loves you for a long, long time, not just to play with, but really loves you, then you become Real."*
>
> *"Does it hurt?" asked the rabbit.*
>
> *"Sometimes" said the Skin Horse, for he was always truthful. "When you are real, you don't mind being hurt."*
>
> *"Does it happen all at once, like being wound up," the rabbit asked, "or bit by bit?"*
>
> *"It doesn't happen all at once," said the Skin Horse. "You become. It takes a long time. That's why it doesn't happen to people who break easily, or have sharp edges, or who have to be carefully kept. Generally by the time you are Real, most of your hair has been loved off, and your eyes drop out, and you get loose in all the joints and very shabby. But these things don't matter at all, because once you are Real you can't be ugly, except to people who don't understand."*

The Skin Horse understood character development.

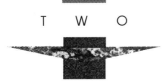

Gaining Fresh Perspective . . . Understanding Perception and Personal Paradigms

"Keep your face to the sunshine and you cannot see the shadows."
HELEN KELLER

"Perception is reality." We hear it a lot. I use the phrase in many of my programs. I don't know the original source to credit. It sounds like a Ben Franklin line to me. But I do know there isan awful lot of truth in it. I love the Helen Keller quote above. Isn't it interesting what a blind person can teach us about perception using visual words? How we see things depends on our perspective. Perhaps it is better said that it depends on our position at the time.

So what exactly does *perception is reality* mean? Simply stated it means that what you (or someone else) think or feel about a certain situation is the way it is in your own mind. Therefore we could say it *is* real (at least to you). It doesn't mean in actuality that what you perceive is true or truth. Perception can't alter real principles or truths as discussed in Chapter 1. But it is important to understand this concept; particularly from an interpersonal perspective.

One of the most common and comical ways we deal with perception every day is when we drive. You have no doubt noticed that when you look into the side view mirrors located just outside your

17

driver and passenger windows, you see two things. Hopefully, the first is other cars beside or behind you. But you probably notice a message as well: *The objects in the mirror are closer than they appear.* Oh yeah, how much closer? What am I supposed to do about it? All I can see is a tiny, little Mac truck running up my rear end, closing fast, and I'm wondering how much closer he really is than he appears. This is a perception problem!

I'll never forget the day Gigi, my wife, came in the house holding a "perception problem" in her hand. We had just moved into a new house and had recently purchased a minivan that she drove. In her hand was the passenger side-view mirror—adjustment cable and all. It seems she perceived the garage was a little wider than it really was. In this case, her perception was *not* reality. (This story used with her reluctant permission.)

For another illustration, let's pick on the politicians like everyone else does. Let's say my perception is that "nothing worthwhile ever gets accomplished in Washington (D.C.)." I mean, just look at all the time and money they waste. What do they do up there anyway? Why in the world do they have all those "staff" people? Why doesn't anything ever get done? (We'll see in a minute that there are several things that affect my perceptions.)

Is my perception of the situation in Washington right? Perhaps. Partially, at least. But not completely. They do get things done sometimes and, occassionally, some very positive things get accomplished, depending of course on your political persuasion (another perception issue). But back to my original statement. Is my perception reality? It is to me. Does it affect the way I vote? Absolutely! Should my representatives and senators be concerned about my perceptions, even if they aren't exactly right? Only if she wants to get re-elected.

I like to use the concept of perception to lead into a discussion of another concept that has received a lot of attention in recent years . . . paradigms. Many of us were introduced to the concept of paradigms and paradigm shifts in the mid-late 80s by Joel Barker and his work presented in *Discovering the Future*. It is the seminal work in this area. If you have not seen this video or are unfamiliar with his work in this area, I strongly suggest you familiarize yourself with it by seeing the video or reading one of his subsequent books.

Let's begin our discussion of the power of paradigms by defining *paradigms* and establishing a base upon which we can build. The Thesaurus lists a few good synonyms for the word to provide the context for further discussion. The synonyms suggested include *model, ideals, patterns and standards.* Let me suggest two additional ones: *grid* and *filter.* So let's put it all together and come up with a good working definition for paradigms.

Paradigms are filters that consist of our personal ideals and standards through which we perceive, understand and interpret our world.

A few examples may help clarify this further. Consider . . .

"the world is flat" view of Columbus' day vs. Columbus' view of the world as round

the Berlin wall vs. the fall of communism in Eastern Europe and the Soviet Union

sales and service as defined by "the company's" vs. how the customer defines them

If it ain't broke, don't fix it vs. the continuous improvement mindset

Have you ever wondered what Columbus' peers and superiors thought about him? Most of them thought he was crazy. Most thought he would fall off the face (edge) of the earth. But Columbus, determined to broaden his horizons (I couldn't resist the pun), even convinced a king to finance the deal! Imagine the crowds he would draw today if he turned whatever he said and did into a "how to negotiate to win" seminar. Imagine the books and tapes he could have sold on Spain's late night TV infomercial channel!

No doubt that in our lifetime one of the most immense, powerful, and life changing paradigm shifts occurred when the Berlin Wall came down after nearly fifty years. Freedom at last for millions of people. But it has been anything but easy. Shifting paradigms never is. As a matter of fact, it has been one of the most difficult human undertakings ever. The reasons and obstacles are too numerous to discuss here. Personal freedom always demands a great price, and it always will.

On the corporate front, we can certainly relate to the last two. Quality and customer focus paradigm shifts have changed, and in some cases, revolutionized the way we do business. We have shifted the ways we perceive and serve our customers, the way we design and deliver products and services, and the way we interface with suppliers. Isn't the change great? Unless of course all this *change* has stressed you out. You see many people are resistant to change, even if it is ultimately for the better. They work hard to protect the *status quo*. We'll examine this in more detail when we discuss personal styles.

These business paradigm shifts described above provide us with the opportunities to conduct business through win/win, empowering, strategic alliances and relationships. So why isn't everyone excited? Ten years after the quality movement began, why are so many organizations disappointed with their results? Why do the other initiatives (continuous improvement, empowerment, employee involvement) lose steam, fade out or lose their flavor (of the month, you might say)? The answers lie in people. One of my *compelling* reasons for writing this book about building people and relationships is that I believe that *people are at the core of the problems and solutions*.

Why is it important to talk about personal paradigms and paradigm shifts? In addition to what I've already said, let me suggest a few more reasons. For me personally, the first reason was simply understanding paradigms: what they are, why they exist, *and* that people tend to get *stuck* in certain types. Another reason, that follows logically, is to understand the need for shifting paradigms to different perspectives based on new understanding or information.

A third reason is that these paradigm shifts may cause you to think differently; modify your approach to relationships, and help us become more successful people and more successful with people.

One of the simple exercises I have used over the years to help people "get it" regarding paradigms and thinking differently is the nine dots exercise. Since people, like yourselves, have become more sophisticated over the years, I changed to the (more sophisticated) sixteen dots exercise. (You know the definition of a sophisticated person. It is a person who hears the *William Tell Overture* and *doesn't* immediately think of the Lone Ranger!)

The sixteen dot exercise as seen in Figure 1 has the same intent as the nine dot one, but it is a little more difficult. For those who haven't seen it before, the answer is provided in the Appendix. I wouldn't be so cruel as to make you call me for the answer or leave you hanging. That would drive some of you over the edge!

You may recall the purpose of the exercise was to get us to "think outside the box." We tend to become limited by self-imposed boundaries and those others impose on us. These boundaries, if you will, inhibit our ability to think freely (differently). We are unable to *think* or *do* outside the lines. Creativity, another hot topic today, is squelched or non-existent. Our personal paradigms may *contain* and *constrain* us.

I'd like to suggest a definition for personal paradigms.

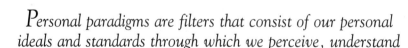

*P*ersonal paradigms are filters that consist of our personal
ideals and standards through which we perceive, understand
and interpret ourselves.

Please notice that I modified the paradigm definition only slightly. The focus here is you and me as individuals. (We'll deal with interpersonal paradigms in the second part of the book.) Understanding personal paradigms and how they affect our lives, can have power-

THE PARADIGM BOX

Use only six straight lines and draw them in a way so that all sixteen dots are connected.

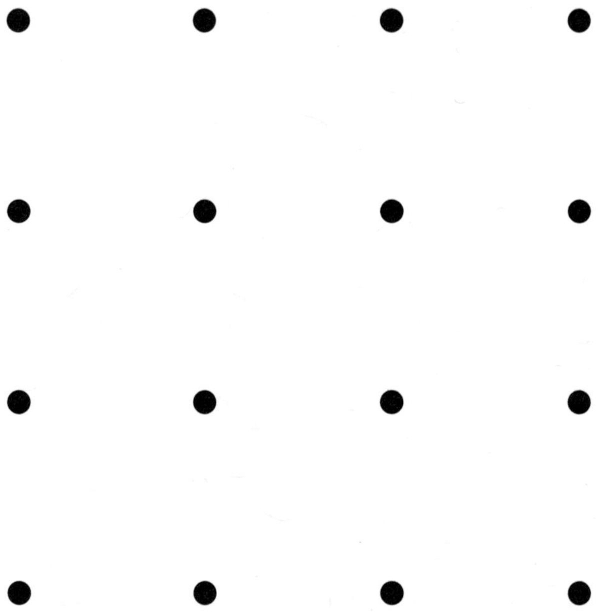

●   ●   ●   ●

●   ●   ●   ●

●   ●   ●   ●

●   ●   ●   ●

Figure 1
Sixteen Dot Paradigm Exercise

ful—even life changing—consequences. And what's more, the changes and consequences are positive ones *if* we use the power tools to help us make the appropriate paradigm shifts and apply them in our personal and professional lives.

PERSONAL PARADIGMS

One of the best tools for discussing expectations is *The Perception and Expectations Wheel* diagram (Figure 2). This represents my adaptation of a diagram that first appeared in *Harvard Business Review* in 1956.[1] Let's examine the wheel by dividing it into two parts: personal paradigms and expectations. The personal paradigms include the pieces *Ideals, Values,* and *Goals & Objectives.*

Ideals may be understood as the way we view people and things. It is the way we think they ought to be or wish they would be. We all have *idealistic* paradigms from which we operate. Ideals represent the way we would design and operate things if we had our own way.

Since there is a chapter dedicated to the discussion of *values,* I will simply state here the definition. *Values are the paradigms of attitudes and standards from which we operate; our sense of right and wrong, or good and bad.* They dramatically affect our perceptions and expectations.

Goals and *objectives* are those things that we want to personally achieve in life. They tend to show how we define success or failure. There is greater discussion of them in Chapter 6 when we look at personal motivation. They are very much related to personal expectations which leads us to the next chapter . . .

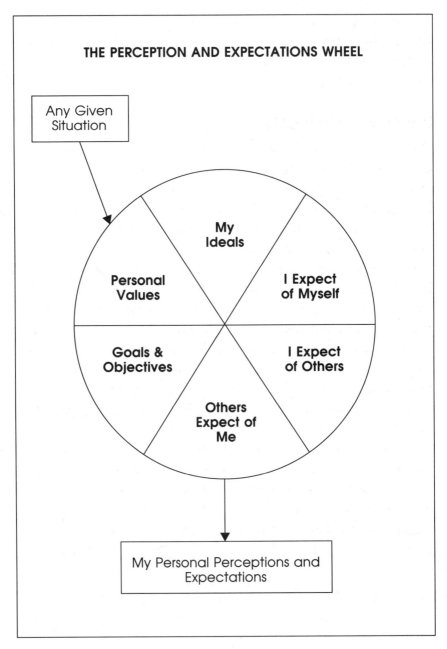

Figure 2

T   H   R   E   E

Setting Myself Up to Succeed or Fail? . . . Managing Personal Expectations

"Blessed is the one who has no expectations,
for he shall not be disappointed."

BEN FRANKLIN

"I thought I would be the last one to be laid off." "I thought I would win." "I thought I would get that promotion." "I thought we would stay together forever." "I never thought I would be the one to get it." Words of disappointment and discouragement. What a somber way to begin a chapter! This is beginning to depress me and I'm writing it. Well hold on; there is a reason for starting out this way. By the time we finish, you will be provided with tools to help you better manage the expectations monster.

So I ask you . . . Why do people fail? Why do relationships fail? Why do businesses fail? A good place to start looking for answers to these questions is EXPECTATIONS. The dictionary defines expectation *as something looked forward to as certain or probable*. There are a couple of clues here. The first is "something looked forward to." When we "look forward to something," we usually have a very positive or even excited anticipation about the expected outcome. And as the second part of the definition implies (as certain or probable), we believe it will or *should* happen.

25

Should. This is where we begin to head for trouble. Should have. Let's conjugate this phrase. *I should have, you should have, she/he should have, we should have, you should have, they should have . . .* Sounds like each person is beginning to start down the primary path that leads to failure for individuals, relationships and businesses . . . *blaming* and *excusing.*

When *should have's* don't happen, people begin to practice two exercises that, if they were aerobic in nature, could rid the world of cardiovascular diseases forever. In the first, they make a fist with their thumb wrapped around it at about ring finger level. Then it happens. They punch other people? No, even more damaging. They release their pointer finger allowing it to fly straight out toward their victim, pointing at the "real reason" for the failure: anyone or anything except themselves. They are the Blamers. It is always someone else's fault.

The second exercise takes a more subtle approach, but just as effective. In this one, the person (let's call her the blamee) takes her chin and slowly drops it toward her chest. For maximum effect, it is often useful to roll the eyes prior to dropping the head. This usually slows down even the most brutal blamer. Once these physical movements are completed, the blamee is free to begin *making excuses* for why whatever was expected to happen didn't or whatever was expected to succeed, failed. They are the Shamers.

Let's examine expectations a little more closely to see how we can avoid the plight of the "blamers and shamers." In order to do so, let's re-visit the *Perception and Expectations Wheel* (Figure 1). This time we want to examine the three pieces in the second half of the wheel. They are related to expectations.

MANAGING PERSONAL EXPECTATIONS

I Expect of Me

The piece "I expect of me" is a personal one. It provides us with the first opportunity to perceive ourselves as a success or failure; to be delighted or disappointed with "me." What will the outcome be? It depends to a large extent on your personal expectations. Are they too high, too low, or non-existent?

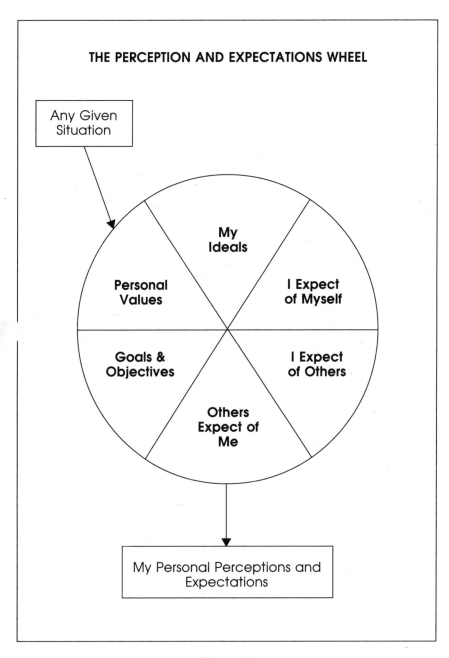

Figure 1

NO EXPECTATIONS

Remember the quote at the beginning of the chapter? "He who hath no expectations shall not be disappointed." This is absolutely true, but what a way to live. Many of us would say this isn't living at all, but someone simply going through the motions of life. It brings to mind a person who is not motivated, bored or apathetic, and takes no pride in themselves. This person typically has a very low self-esteem and what little motivation they have is simply to "get by."

They are, however, capable of playing the role of blamer or shamer in their personal and professional lives. As an example, consider Jack, a young man in his mid-twenties with no real expectations of himself. His indifferent attitude and inability to make a commitment to anything or anyone cause problems on both fronts. On the personal side, his inability to make a commitment to one person leads to his girlfriend breaking off their relationship. He reasons that he didn't ask her for a commitment, why should she ask one from him? So he moves on from one shallow, short-term relationship to another.

At work, these same attitude problems lead to poor performance, and Jack finally loses his job. He reasons that he didn't really like that job much anyway and moves on to another, and another, etc. You get the picture. People like Jack who have no expectations and "don't have to worry about being disappointed" are usually always disappointed. It comes in two flavors.

The first is disappointment with themselves. They reason to themselves that "I never did anything right anyway" or "I'm just stupid." They are classic *shamers*. The second is disappointment with others. They are always holding others responsible for "never giving them a chance" or "cutting them a break." They are the classic *blamers*.

LOW EXPECTATIONS

People with low expectations typically set themselves up to "win" (at least in their own minds). They aim low intentionally because it is easier to hit the target. In so doing, they avoid the disappointment of not meeting or living up to their own expectations. They are more motivated than people like Jack (their "no expectation" counterpart), but very *risk aversive*. They *fear being wrong* or criticized more than they feel good about being right or at least having tried. They tend to be very satisfied with the *status quo*.

These characteristics carry over into personal and professional settings. On the personal side, the impact isn't all that dramatic because they tend to be comfortable with things as they are. Consider Martha, a mid-level manager for a telecommunications company. At home, she isn't interested in winning awards for the best lawn and garden or setting records in any 10K races. There is nothing *wrong* with her approach. She basically has a "live and let live" mentality. She works hardest at keeping things pretty much the same.

This carries over to work as well. Her only professional goals are to do her job well enough to keep her job. She has no aspirations of "moving up the ladder" because she doesn't want the accompanying risks and headaches. Left to her own plans, she sets sales targets with plenty of cushion. Sound familiar? We will see more potentially dramatic results and consequences from this low expectation attitude when we re-visit Martha later in this chapter in the section *What I Expect From Others*.

"GREAT EXPECTATIONS"

When expectations are too high, people have generally set themselves up to fail. The primary accompanying negative result is *frustration*. It isn't hard to understand why someone would become frustrated if they never met or lived up to their own expectations. Who wouldn't? We have heard well-meaning "experts" encourage us to "shoot for the stars or always set your goals just outside your grasp so you'll keep trying harder."

Most people like the sense of accomplishment of actually reaching a personal goal or meeting their own expectation. Those whose expectations are too high never seem to quite get there, and thus they end up frustrated.

Meet Bob, a director of engineering for an aerospace company. He is a highly motivated, driven individual who has lofty goals and expectations. This sounds good to me. So what is the problem? Bob is frustrated on all fronts. On the personal side, Bob is a jogger. He decided he wanted to run his next 10K race in under 40 minutes. That sounds reasonable enough you say. But, he has never run one in under 52 minutes and has had little time for training due to his recently hectic travel schedule.

If you are a runner, you know that cutting nearly 2 minutes per mile off your time is pretty incredible. Success is highly unlikely in Bob's case unless the course is all downhill, the wind stays at his back, or he puts menthol sports creme in his athletic supporter!

At work, Bob also has lofty expectations. He expects to be a vice-president for the company one day. Tomorrow is soon enough. After all, he is imminently more qualified than the others considered to be potential executive timbre. The problem is Bob is a "legend in his own mind" around the office. He has little peer respect and hasn't performed that well in current and past assignments. Set up to fail? Probably so, unless his dad is the CEO!

What I Expect of Others

We have seen how personal expectations can lead to potentially difficult circumstances and results that disappoint or frustrate. Expectations play an even larger role when we take the next giant step and involve *other people*. Some of us would rather not do this, while others of us thrive on relationships with other people.

Let's now shift the perspective from expectations of ourselves to *what I expect of others*. Here lies another great opportunity for personal growth. Consider again Martha who has low personal expectations as described previously. When it comes to her kids, she believes and trusts that they are doing the best they can. She accepts the grades her children bring home on their report cards as the best they can do. However, test scores indicate differently.

Her teenage son has tested out with a very high aptitude in math, yet continues to get, at best, average grades. Does she dare ask why and "risk" the possibility of upsetting him or causing a confrontation? Surely she couldn't probe the issue and challenge him to raise his own level of expectations, could she? After all, he is doing better than passing with his average grades. Her own low expectations are passed along to her son who may not reach his potential because no one ever challenged him to do so.

On the work side, Martha manages a department of sales people with varying abilities. (What department doesn't have these?) As mentioned previously, when she is able to, she sets her sales targets low to insure they are met. She *hates* annual performance review time. (Most managers do. She is the one I referred to in the introduction of this book who would prefer to do performance reviews via voice mail.) She usually rates everyone about the same regardless of level of performance because it seems less risky. Her low expectations bring down the overall performance level and morale in her entire department. Her approach keeps low performers low, average performers average, and (here is the worst part) brings high performers down. The latter doesn't last however.

Whew! That's good you say. No, the high performers won't stay down, but the problem is they won't stay at all. They leave! They are typically too motivated to work in the kind of environment that managers like Martha create.

Let's visit Bob again; good old "see you at the top leaving footprints on your back" Bob. At home, Bob continuously goes for the Guinness record each time he mows his lawn. He can play a round of golf in under three hours. He does this by hitting into people in front of him until they let him "play through" and he never "putts out." With his kids he is also very demanding. He expects that they will make the honor roll and really lets them have it when they don't. He expects them to "excel" in all that they do, sports included. He wonders why they really don't hang around much when they don't have to; why they don't want to do things together with him.

At work, Bob also expects those working FOR him to put in the same demanding schedule he does. After all, if he puts in long hours, why shouldn't everyone else? He also expects things to get completed yesterday. He expects people to go the extra mile like he does, no matter what it takes. Trouble ahead.

When we pile our expectations onto someone else's plate, we open the door to several exciting possibilities; only one of which is positive. The positive one is that someone steps up, accepts our pile, and actually meets our expectations. When this happens, everyone is satisfied, right? Wrong. The "too high" expectation person is satisfied for an infinitesimal moment, and then asks one of his favorite questions, "What have you done for me lately?" Who is disappointed and frustrated? Everyone. When my expectations of myself are so high that I can't meet them, how can other people meet them? They can't. Set up to fail? You bet.

What Others Expect of Me

In this instance, the perspective again shifts. This time we focus on "what others expect of me." Just like I have expectations of others, other people have certain expectations of me. I have to come to grips with these expectations whether high or low. Then I must determine whether or not I *choose* to meet or perform to their level of expectation. The key word is *choose*. It is a choice for most of us; a trap for others.

The *choice* involves deciding whether or not I believe meeting someone else's expectations is congruent with my personal values and goals. If they are, I will attempt to meet them only up to my own level of personal motivation. Beyond that level, I choose not to do so unless there are externally motivating factors, e.g. survival, mega-bucks, etc.

The *trap* involves those who can't really make their own choices. They feel compelled to meet any and all expectations. The reasons vary from complicated dysfunctional relationships to simply being a "people pleaser."

LET'S GET REAL

How do we proactively manage expectations to create win/win situations, both personally and inter-personally? I suggest there are three tools for managing both sets of expectations.

Reality Checks

Setting expectations not too low, not too high, but realistic for you based on who you are, and where you are in your personal and professional life. They also depend on external factors, some of which are going to be outside of your control.

How do you set realistic expectations? I offer two suggestions at this point. The first is *read on*. Finish the book. One of my goals throughout the rest of the first part of the book is to equip you with the tools to better understand yourself (strengths, weaknesses, roles, motivations, etc.) so that you can return to this later to assess the "reality" of your expectations.

The second *how to* is ASK! Ask someone with the following qualifications: someone who knows you well; someone who is interested in your well-being/has your best interest at heart; someone whose input you would highly regard; someone you trust. You may not find someone who meets all the above, but this will get you started. So get started!

Control

This is big. This is huge. This is MEGA! Who has control? Are your expectations within your control or do they depend on someone or something else *outside your control*. We waste so much time and energy expecting things to happen to us or for us when we have *no control* over the situation. When it doesn't happen? Anger, frustration, disappointment, etc. For example, the recent rash of airline tragedies calls to mind for me, a semi-nervous flier, that I expect to take off and land safely each time I board a plane. However, the reality is I don't control much, if any, of what happens. If I get my pilot's license and fly myself, then I think I am in more control. But even here I am not totally in control because I am at the mercy of the equipment and those who build and repair it.

Another example. I wanted to start my own company at some point in time. I did so about four years ago. I controlled most of the essentials, e.g. quit what I was doing previously, took some of our money out of the bank, took some more of our money out of the bank, and then got a loan to take some of their money out of the bank. (You get the picture.) The point is it was totally my decision (provided Gigi, my wife, was in agreement). I controlled all that was necessary to make this goal a reality.

So who's in control anyway? Before proceeding you need to know that I believe in a personal, sovereign God, who ultimately controls all things. (This is a personal values statement. Values will be addressed in the next chapter.) Whether you agree with that statement or not isn't the issue here. The issue is there are circumstances and things that other people control. There are also things I pretty much control and about which I have to make choices. How successful we are in managing personal and professional expectations depends to a great extent on *who has control*. We need to concentrate on and develop these expectations around things primarily within our own control.

Ownership

A few months back, I was discussing this whole issue of expectations, disappointment, frustration, etc. with a close friend of mine who meets the qualifications mentioned above. I really trust this man and highly value his input and opinion. He gave me a good thought to build on the two points we just discussed. (Reality and control.) His word was *ownership*. Who owns the expectation? This is particularly important as it relates to inter-personal expectations. It is one thing to expect something of yourself. It is something different altogether when the expectation is transferred to someone else.

Your expectations may seem realistic from your point of view. They may even appear that way to the other person as well. But the issue now becomes one of *ownership*. Whose expectation is it? Who owns it? If I still own it and can't convince someone else to own it with me or get buy-in, it remains still only my expectation. The other person didn't accept ownership of it. So unless I adjust it, modify it, or in some way re-package it so they will own it, I am the only one hoping this expectation gets met. Thus the possibility again exists that my expectations may go unmet. In many cases, this leads to personal or interpersonal disappointment and frustration. Failure to clarify and transfer ownership of expectations may set ourselves and others up to fail.

F   O   U   R

Valuing Values . . .
The Role of Personal
Values in Your Life

*"That which we obtain too easily, we esteem too lightly;
it is dearness only that gives everything its value."*

THOMAS PAINE

Want to start an argument? Begin by discussing one or more of the following: religion, politics, racial issues, individual rights, capital punishment, the role of the media, the state of education in our nation, or any controversial issue about which people have strong beliefs and opinions. Why do many conversations concerning these subjects end up in arguments? *Values.* More specifically, *personal values.* Mark Twain said it well, "The rule is perfect. In all matters of opinion, our adversaries are insane."

This chapter will be fairly short because there are fewer ways to stir people up and have them walk out of a room (or close a book) than to start a discussion of values. My guess is some were tempted to shut down on me in the chapter on *character* because I used some stories from the Bible, and they were personally offended. Sorry. I can't control your emotions or response to what I write. Only you can do that. I use (as do most authors and speakers) different sources of information that I believe to be credible. These sources come from various places. They are based in fact, and when personal opinion is interjected, it is noted as just that . . . opinion.

Others might suggest that things needs to be *politically correct.* Again, sorry. Political correctness, as I understand it and have seen it demonstrated, is more a representation of *valuelessness* than anything to come along since *situational* ethics in the 70s. Both are sorely lacking in any basis of character and principle. (Some would say this is my value judgment.) See how you can get someone started?

The purpose of this chapter is not to stir you up or even make value judgments. It is not to convince you that my values need to be yours. While I will share some of my personal values to help illustrate a few points a bit later, I am not proselyting. (I provided this warning so that you can skip those parts if you choose.) Back to the purpose. The purpose of this chapter is to help you better understand personal values, examine your own, and provide a couple of exercises to help you sort some things out. If you don't understand your personal values and are unable to articulate them, no one else will understand them either.

Before going further in our discussions of understanding personal values, let's make sure you understand how I am defining them.

Values are paradigms of beliefs and convictions from which we make judgments and choices, and that strongly influence our behaviors and attitudes.

In Chapter 1, we said that *character* addresses the *who we really are* questions. *Values* address the *why we do what we do* questions. *Why* issues deal with our *motives* for doing what we do. From our paradigms of values, we judge right/wrong or good/bad and make choices accordingly. You can see why these *values issues* can be so "hot." I'm right, you're wrong. That's good, that's bad. Clearly the answer is this or how can you possibly think it is that? Etc.

Hopefully this definition makes understanding the importance of personal values more obvious. I recognize that some of you are thinking two fairly common thoughts regarding values. The first is *Why is understanding values important in the first place?* My usual response is that old tried and true accounting answer . . . it depends! It depends how well you want to know and understand yourself, and how much you value relationships (the focus of the second part of the book).

The second thought some of you may have is "personal values are just that . . . personal. So leave mine alone. They should remain private and not be discussed openly." If the environment is right, my experience is that most people are willing, and some even want, to talk about their values.

Part of the context of this experience is from those programs I deliver in which the participants engage in values clarification exercises similar to the one that you will find later in this chapter. The other experience is simply that of my own personal and business relationships. I believe one very good reason to understand your personal values is to determine if they align with those of your place of occupation and people with whom you work and spend your life.

It is very difficult to work at a place where the corporate values are out of alignment with your own personal values. (I don't necessarily mean the values as printed on the corporate reports and banners. I mean the ones they actually abide by. Unfortunately there is often a difference.)

Let's say, for example, you are an animal rights activist and your company develops medical products. Pre-clinical testing requires significant animal testing to demonstrate safety and efficacy. (I use this example as I spent over fifteen years in the medical device industry.) You believe this testing isn't necessary and is also inhumane to animals. Can you continue to work with this organization or in this industry? Do you continuously turn in your own company to the authorities for what you consider to be violations? It is a value judgment on your part. Which do you value more: your position on animal rights or your position with the company?

A recent, somewhat similar, situation in the Pacific Northwest arose over protecting the spotted owl versus jobs in the lumber industry. There are strong feelings on both sides. Why? Very different values. My personal opinion is . . . (No way I'm getting into that here. I said I wasn't trying to stir things up!)

Another important aspect of personal values is alignment. Personal alignment may be defined as alignment of character, values and behaviors. When these are aligned, our *personal operating system* functions in a path of "least resistance" so to speak. When any of these three are out of synch, we are, in a sense, working against ourselves. It requires more energy to do so and typically causes more stress.

ORIGIN OF PERSONAL VALUES

Where do our values come from? How do we get them? Let me suggest three things that strongly develop and influence our values: *people*, *environment*, and *experience*.

People

Without a doubt the most dominant source of values development comes from your parents or whoever spent the most time raising you. Whether it was one parent, both, a grandparent or relatives, these people most significantly affect our values in the early stages of development. The next would probably be the teachers, other relatives, friends and neighbors with whom you spent the most time. Time is the key element.

We are probably at our best as students when we are very young. Consider the most often asked question of our little ones. "Why?" "Why, daddy?" "Why, mommy?" And then their follow-up question that comes right after our answer . . . "Why?"

Getting back to the time element for a minute, consider the following. If time with our children is one of, if not, the primary factor influencing values, we need to ask ourselves how much time is spent with our children. I'm not going to accept the cop-out that you spend quality time versus quantity. They need both. Quantity is important.

I could say the same about my golf swing. If I said I want to be a great golfer, then I would have to hit hundreds of balls a day; thousands a week. I couldn't get by focusing just on the quality aspect. But I don't have the time to be a great golfer. Therefore I have to make trade-offs because there are things higher on my priority list than hitting my golf ball into the trees on the right instead of the trees on the left. (I'm a left-handed golfer, and if I did that it would mean I cured my slice by developing a hook.) Anything we want to master takes time and many repetitions. The same is true of being a good spouse and parent.

Like many of you other men, two of my highest priority goals are to be a great husband and dad. I work hard at it, and still have a long way to go. (Just ask my family!) In order to accomplish these lofty goals, a lot of time is required. Early in my career, I was able to spend tremendous amounts of time at work because I was single and didn't have as many responsibilities. Now that I am married, have three very active children and my own company, making time to achieve these personal goals and maintain my priorities requires a lot of effort and commitment.

A quick *time audit* will go a long way towards helping us see where our priorities are based on where our time is spent. A time audit is where you sit down with your time management planner or calendar and see where you spent your time during that week or month. Obviously, when you subtract work and sleep hours, there aren't many left to manage.

Let's say you live in a metro area, and it takes about an hour from the time you walk out of your house until you walk in the office. If you work an average day, this accounts for about ten hours including lunch, etc. If you only sleep an average of seven hours, you are left with about five hours to do everything else including eating your breakfast and dinner at home. Those who travel extensively have an even more difficult time of it.

The question is "Can you accomplish your personal goals in that time period?" If yes, then you're in enviable shape. If not, what will you change, if anything? *Our values determine our priorities.* If an imbalance exists between our values (priorities) and where we spend our time, our stress level will increase. (Our "feeling guilty" level will as well.) We all need balance in our lives to keep healthy. Learning to maintain this balance is another book.

Environment

This is the second values development factor. It actually overlaps to a certain extent with people. *Environment* has to do with the surroundings we grow up in or where we spend the most time. There's that *time* word again. This has little to do with wealth, race, and gender. It doesn't matter much if you're rich or poor, black or white, male or female.

Character and values transcend all of these. We all know stories of individuals who overcame tremendous social disadvantages and/or racial prejudices to become men and women of outstanding character, living out their values in very influential ways. We also know the flip side, where the wealthy kid who had it all (perhaps that was the problem) ended up in serious trouble due to irresponsible behavior. Recently, the media has featured several "famous" examples.

What kind of environment are we trying to create to foster character and values? While the examples are primarily aimed at our children, you may want to consider how these also parallel what is needed to create the *corporate culture* many strive for today.

ENVIRONMENT #1—CARING

This is the most important. We love each other and express it openly and frequently. We are quick with a hug or pat on the back. We also care enough to discipline each child according to his or her needs and personal style. In the early years, that does include spanking as a last resort, not a primary response. We believe Solomon's admonition "spare the rod and spoil the child." Discipline comes out of love, not anger. *One size does not fit all.*

We demonstrate our caring concern for others through our prayers, giving and service. We work hard on this one because while we are not wealthy people, we have been blessed more than some and are committed to being good stewards of what we have. That means sharing it to help meet the needs of others. Children need to learn this early. It really is—no fooling, absolutely, positively *more blessed to give than to receive*. But do our kids see this? Are our *walk* and *talk* in alignment?

ENVIRONMENT #2—COMMUNICATION

We attempt to communicate openly and honestly with each other. This is tough to do. Some of us communicate more loudly and frequently than others. Those of us who fall into this category need to be great learners. Hopefully, we have learned a lot about humility, and learning to say we're sorry—a difficult thing to do for prideful people.

I learned something from Dr. Howard Hendricks a number of years ago. He discussed a concept that all married couples would do well to learn. Briefly stated, it has to do with praising your spouse in front of the kids. This simple practice does wonders for helping them see examples of healthy, positive reinforcement. They certainly see enough of the opposite from us and others.

In addition to praising my wife in front of the kids, another thing I learned from Dr. Hendricks is the practice of periodically reminding my kids how glad I am to be their dad. They need to hear this stuff from us, especially us dads. We men still seem to have more problems with being transparent and open in relationships. I'm not writing this to address the *why*, but to suggest you just start doing things like these if you want to significantly influence your kids' values.

All of us need to encourage our kids to say what they think and try not to squelch their feelings. They need an outlet for anger and frustration, just like we do. Everyone has to dump their bucket at times. The key with our kids is to teach them to *communicate with respect*. This is a tough assignment and like anything else takes a commitment of time.

If we did a better job with this *communicating with respect* issue with the people in our organizations, we would be doing fewer communication and conflict resolution programs.

ENVIRONMENT #3—COURAGE
Gigi and I haven't gotten as far along with this one with our children as many of you because our children are still pretty young. Courage to stand up for what is right and the principles they hold dear. Courage to defend the oppressed and their personal freedoms. Courage to try new ways of doing things. Courage to try and fail and try again. Courage to admit when they're wrong and say so. Courage to work through and manage adversity. Courage to be all they were created to be in both the being and doing sides of their character. Courage to pursue their personal life goals.

Experience
Oscar Wilde said "Experience is the name everyone gives to their mistakes." Most of us can identify with this at times. We believe experience is a great teacher when the experience was, for the most part, positive. And we feel fate has dealt with us unfairly when the experience is bad. The real question is have we learned from our experience? What have we learned? Consider the lesson shared in Mark Twain's words of wisdom.

"We should be careful to get out of an experience only the wisdom that is in it—and stop there; lest we be like the cat that sits down on a hot stove lid. She will never sit down on a hot stove lid again—and that is well, but also she will never sit down on a cold one anymore."

Do experiences impact our values? Can they shape or change our values? The answers to both are yes, but they come in different ways based on our age and maturity level. In our early, formative years, we are sponges in terms of learning from people, environments and experiences. Young children learn better from experiences than most adults. Children tend to be more teachable and impressionable. Values lessons are included. Consider the hot stove quote above. In addition to teaching, children learn values from what some would consider negative experiences like discipline, failure, and disappointment.

Some who write on the subject of values submit that once we mature through adolescence into early adulthood, values usually do not change. The exception, it is suggested, is the traumatic or emotional life changing experience. These experiences include things like death of a loved one, a divorce or family break-up, unexpected loss of a job/unemployment, a religious conversion experience, and so on.

Experience, indeed, can be a great teacher and molder of values. Experiences, as we said before, come in positive and negative flavors. Ask yourself these questions. Can I turn negative experiences into positive learning opportunities? Can I use them to reinforce and strengthen my values rather than cause me to compromise or move away from them? And remember the key words that keep recurring. *It takes time.*

A FINAL WORD ON VALUES

For those of you with quantitative minds who like to measure things, I offer this for your consideration. I once heard someone suggest that if you want a way to measure what you value most, look in your checkbook. Thumb through the register or (if you are like us and keep it all on computer), boot up the money management software on your personal computer. Click on the checkbook, and page down through your transactions. Run the report that prints out expenses by category. Examine the totals and where your money is spent. Keep in mind the words of one who epitomized impeccable character and love for others . . . *"where your treasure is, there will your heart be also."*

To help you sort out your thinking with regard to personal values, following is a values clarification exercise. I believe it can help you process some of the information I provided in this chapter. Again, the primary objective is to get you to spend some time sorting out your personal values.

PERSONAL VALUES CLARIFICATION EXERCISE

Following is a list of personal values statements. While it is not exhaustive, it does contain values statements covering many areas of our lives. To help clarify your own personal values, complete the following exercise designed to help you focus on what is most important to you.

Personal Values Statement	Top 10	Top 5	Number 1
Accomplish personal goals			
Accomplish work goals			
Advancement/promotion up ladder of success (work)			
Financial security			
Maintaining character/integrity			
Personal happiness			
Building and maintaining family relationships			
Building and maintaining personal relationships (friends)			
Religion/personal relationship with God			
Contributing to the betterment of society			
Power (either control or influence or both)			
Personal health and fitness			
Recreation and hobbies			
Environmental responsibility			
World peace			
Other (list your own here, not included above)			

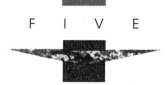

F I V E

Uniquely Created to Be You
. . . Personal Style Issues

"Many receive advice, only the wise profit from it."

SYRUS

When someone asks me to choose the most important *key to success with people*, I think back over the last twenty years or so of professional life and feel compelled to say "understanding personal styles." Based on personal life experiences as a husband, dad, friend and neighbor, I still choose the same. In addition to personal experience, this observation is also based on what I have learned from the organizations for whom I have worked and the thousands of people with whom I have spoken across the country.

So what do I mean by the phrase *understanding personal style?* The simplest way for me to understand and explain it is as follows: personal style describes *needs-based behaviors of normal people that typically provide insight into what they do, how they do it, and why they do it.* Another way of saying it (in jargon) is "how someone is wired."

I threw in a word that may have a few of us a little nervous right now. The word is *normal.* How am I defining *normal people?* The dictionary defines normal as *conforming to a standard considered as usual or typical; natural.* Permit me to provide a layman's definition because I am not a behavioral psychologist or psychiatrist. I am a husband, dad and businessman who happens to have spent much of his life working with and studying people.

I am defining normal here as *people like us*. You know. Those of us with our little personality quirks and minor dysfunctions (admit it, we're all dysfunctional to some extent) who, for the most part, enjoy our lives, our work and other people from time to time. We typically don't consider chainsaws and double-headed axes among our favorite toys. And while we may talk about mounting heat seeking missiles on our cars to deal with jerks in traffic, we usually don't follow through with it. Usually.

To help people understand personal styles, I want to introduce you to (or review with you) a very powerful tool. Many of us are familiar with the various four factor models used today in assessment instruments dealing with needs and behaviors. Allow me to provide you with a little background information on the origin and development behind the four primary personal styles that make up many of the four factor models.

Believe it or not, Hippocrates (circa 400 B.C.) described these four styles in terms of blood, phlegm, black and yellow bile. He used the words choleric, sanguine, phlegmatic, and melancholy to describe *temperaments* of people. Much of the more "current" research regarding the four behavioral styles came from two sources—Carl Jung's work *Psychological Types* and Dr. William Moulton Marston's *The Emotions of Normal People*, both written in the 1920's.

Significant contribution was made in terms of instrument design and development by Dr. John Geier in the 60s. His work developed the particular profile that I use most often. There are obviously numerous other researchers and contributors who have developed these and similar concepts in various ways. Several have started companies that develop and market these products under various names and labels.

My goal here was simply to provide for you a very brief overview of the origin of the personal style four factor models. The ones cited here are those with which I am most familiar, based on the tools I use in my own work with people and organizations. When I am not writing or speaking, part of my time is spent consulting in the quality and re-engineering arenas. Invariably this leads to developing "in-house" programs that address the human side of the success equation, i.e. leadership, teaming, empowerment, conflict, etc. When we started the company, it was necessary to choose a model around which I could design and deliver those program segments dealing with people's *behaviors* and *needs*. Having been exposed to many such tools and models during my own extensive corporate career, I chose to use the DISC-based tools available from several organizations including my own.

Over the years, these tools have served me, and more importantly, my clients, well in terms of the four key measures of success of such instruments: quality, reliability, accuracy and cost/investment. The information and insights that may be gained from these can serve as power tools for success in your personal and professional lives.

I want to introduce you to a simple discovery process I developed that will help you examine your predominant personal style needs/behaviors. To do so, we first need to understand a few things. The primary purpose of the process is to *help you understand you.* Secondly, as we describe the various styles and combinations of styles, please know there are no right/wrong, good/bad, pass/fail, win/lose styles as outcomes. The outcome is simply a capsulized description of your personal needs and behaviors. As mentioned previously, the information gained from this process can provide significant insights to help you improve and even master the art of building relationships, beginning with yourself.

Another important aspect (to me personally) is the freedom that comes from knowing I was uniquely created and gifted with a certain personal style (or combination of styles). Knowing this, we need not spend our time worrying about trying to be like someone else —someone we aren't. *We waste far too much energy pursuing what we are not, rather than enjoying who we are.* We should be free to spend our time *working from* our strengths and *working on* the weaknesses. Knowing and understanding these can bring peace of mind in these areas.

It is probably obvious to you from the chapter title, that I am one of those people who believe that we are born with a predisposition toward our personal style. I recognize there are others who disagree and that's OK. There can be no doubt that environment influences these styles, and in some cases, significantly so.

I believe with all my heart that we (all of us) were **created on purpose for a purpose**. That belief is powerful! It charges and recharges my batteries. A significant part of our life's journey is discovering that purpose and living it out. It also adds FUN to the process, something we all can use more of from time to time.

Whether your theology agrees with mine or not is not the point of this chapter. Hopefully we can agree (or I can persuade you) that understanding personal style issues can lead to personal and interpersonal success. Consider these tools as the batteries to start the understanding personal styles process *or* your jumper cables to give you a *jump-start* if you've "seen this stuff before."

DETERMINING YOUR PERSONAL STYLE

Determining your personal style involves a process that asks you several questions related to personal style issues. They are HOW and WHAT questions that help identify dominant behavioral tendencies, needs, and personal preferences.

Circle the group of words listed below that best describes how you approach things or like things done, e.g. how you work, how you talk, your movements.

Fast/Spontaneous/Hurried   Slow/Planned/Deliberate

If you circled the *fast/spontaneous/hurried* group, put an "X" above the line in Figure 1. If you circled the *slow/planned/deliberate* group, put the "X" below the line.

Now this time we will address the "WHAT" questions. For example, what is your preference relative to "doing" (task-related things) versus "people" (relationships). What would you rather spend your time with: people or projects? Do you say "I can't stand being alone" or "I'd rather be alone"? In Figure 2, place your "X" on the right side of the solid line if you most identify with that group of statements

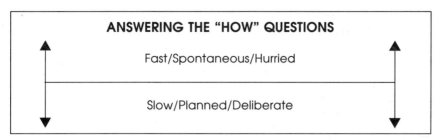

Figure 1

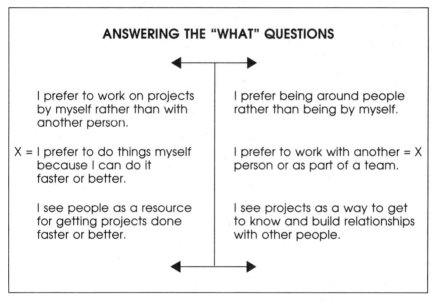

Figure 2

and on the left of the solid line if you most identify with that group of statements.

The final piece is simply combining the two figures BUT still having only one "X". Figure 3 shows this combination. As you can see, the crossing lines now form four quadrants and your "X" should only be in one of them, i.e. top right, top left, bottom right, or bottom left.

COMBINING THE "HOW AND WHAT" QUESTIONS

Fast/spontaneous/hurried

and

Prefer to work on projects
by myself rather than with
another person.

X = Prefer to do things myself
because I can do it
faster or better.

See people as a resource
for getting projects done
faster or better.

Fast/spontaneous/hurried

and

Prefer being around people
rather than being by myself.

Prefer to work with another = X
person or as part of a team.

See projects as a way to get
to know and build relationships
with other people.

Slow/planned/deliberate

and

Prefer to work on projects
by myself rather than with
another person.

X = Prefer to do things myself
because I can do it
faster or better.

See people as a resource
for getting projects done
faster or better.

Slow/planned/deliberate

and

Prefer being around people
rather than being by myself.

Prefer to work with another = X
person or as part of a team.

See projects as a way to get
to know and build relationships
with other people.

Figure 3

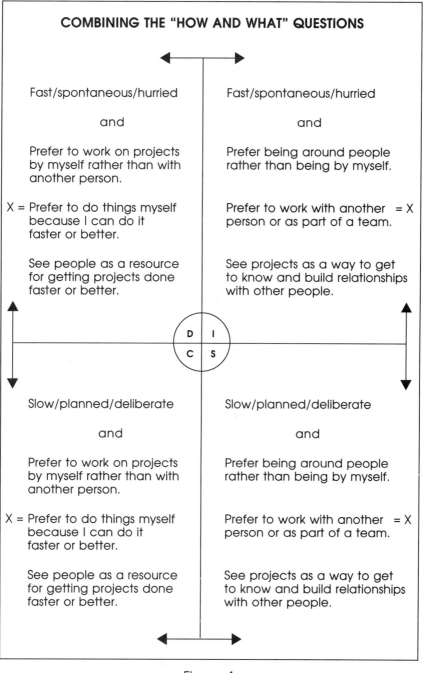

Figure 4
Associating "handles" with the four quadrants

Figure 4 goes one step further. It provides a "handle" for each of the four quadrants so you can *grab* the information specific to each quadrant. I believe this facilitates learning and long term memory to store this information for future use. It is simply easier to remember a letter or word than *sets of* letters and words.

The more we develop each quadrant, the more likely it is that you will begin to think you could fit into more than one quadrant. Let me assure you, you probably do. The remainder of this chapter clarifies and expands on each of these four *styles.* As I do so, you will identify with behaviors or needs in two, three or even all four quadrants. The purpose of the process is not to pigeon hole you into one style. Quite the opposite is true. While many people identify strongly with one dominant style, the objective is for you to develop a personal profile with which you really identify.

Following are descriptions of the four primary personal style needs/behaviors. Key characteristics and attributes of each are discussed so that you may develop a personal profile of yourself as mentioned previously. In addition, a composite chart has been prepared for your use. (See Figure 5.) As you work through each style, highlight or underline those characteristics that you believe most accurately describe yourself.

In order to keep you from developing a profile of your *ideal* person rather than who you really are, a good *checkpoint* is to have your husband/wife, or a good, trusted friend review it and note any differences in their perception versus your own. Sometimes even the best of us suffer from what I call the "legend in our own mind" syndrome.

One thing to keep in mind as we begin this analysis of personal styles is that this section of the book deals only with personal/self issues. We will examine the inter-personal issues of style in detail in Chapter 10.

The High "D"

Direct, determined, decisive, and *doers* are four key "D" words that best describe you if this is your dominant style.

UNDERSTANDING PERSONAL STYLES—NEEDS & BEHAVIORS

"D" Words
1. Direct
2. Determined
3. Decisive
4. Doer

Key Strengths
1. Results-Oriented
2. Confident

Key Weakness
1. Impatient
2. High Control

Fears: Loss of Control

Stress Release
Physical Activity

"I" Words
1. Influence
2. Inspiring
3. Impulsive
4. Interactive

Key Strengths
1. Persuasive
2. Optimistic

Key Weakness
1. Disorganized
2. Talks too much

Fears: Loss of Status

Stress Release
"Dumps their bucket"—
Express emotions/feelings

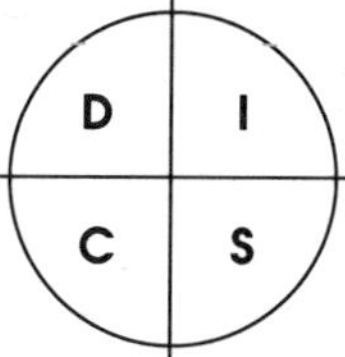

D	**I**
C	**S**

"C" Words
1. Conscientious
2. Cautious
3. Careful
4. Critical

Key Strengths
1. Analytical
2. High Standards

Key Weakness
1. Perfectionist Tendencies
2. Slow to act/decide

Fears: Being wrong;
criticism of their work

Stress Release
Time alone to reason
things out

"S" Words
1. Supportive
2. Steady
3. Sympathetic
4. Status quo

Key Strengths
1. Loyal
2. Team Player

Key Weakness
1. Resistant to change
2. Slow to act/decide

Fears: Change

Stress Release
Times alone to sleep it off

Figure 5
Personal Styles Composite Chart

STRENGTHS

High D's possess an incredible ability to **do.** They can accomplish more in the first two hours of a work day than many people do in a full day. Why? Because more than anything else, they are energized by *results.* Getting results, personal challenge, and attacking problems are a few of their *felt needs.*

Another real strength that dovetails their ability to get results is their high level of self-confidence. No lack of ego here. This combined with a determined spirit drives them to accomplish more. They are willing to take on new challenges and pioneer new areas. They also process information rapidly, and thus are quick decision makers.

Perhaps you have noticed something interesting when you do an analysis of strengths and weaknesses of a particular person or thing. Once the list of strengths is completed, the list of weaknesses becomes almost obvious. The latter are strengths taken to an extreme. Charles Boyd, an author and friend of mine, says it like this, "Weaknesses are simply strengths overextended." So with that, let's examine how the High D turns strengths into weaknesses.

WEAKNESSES

One of the primary problems that High D's face is an outgrowth of their direct, determined, decisive and doer mindset. It is impatience. High D's don't do lines (at least not very well); not at the grocery store or in traffic. They simply want to be doing something or keep moving. Consider Jack, our High D friend. He is easily spotted in rush hour traffic. He is the guy who drives in the emergency lanes or in the carpool lanes even if he is the only one in the car. He may even own an inflatable passenger to ride with him during those times.

Because he is so direct, at times he really offends people with his bluntness. Usually it isn't on purpose. Usually. There are those times that Jack arrives at the office at 8:00 am and by 8:05 no one is speaking to him. That's when you know your D is too high.

Believe it or not they get impatient with themselves if they don't think they are doing something fast enough or getting enough things done. They can become so focused on doing that they become compulsive doers. They feel they have to be doing something all the time. The word *relaxing* isn't in their vocabulary. So most of their hobbies involve doing. Jack thinks of a nice quiet evening out with his wife as dinner and some "slam" dancing!

If a High D has those high, unrealistic expectations referred to earlier, you see how he is set up to fail. He has scheduled more *to do's* than can possibly be done and thus becomes very impatient and frustrated with himself. The High D's self-esteem is strongly tied to his ability to achieve or produce results. If not balanced properly, this becomes a natural *performance trap* and the self-esteem goes up and down according to performance. We'll talk more about performance traps when we examine the High C.

Another area of weakness for the High D is control. They really want to control their environment from the agenda of meetings at work to the schedule around their houses. You know those thermostats on the office walls that have been covered with clear plastic lock boxes? High D's either demand a key or pry those suckers off the wall, and adjust the temperature to their liking. And typically they like it at least 10° colder than anyone else. You can always recognize their secretaries. They are ones whose skin is a pale blue, wear gloves at their desk, and have a space heater under it!

While this High Control tendency produces more problems on the interpersonal side (we'll address those later), it also poses some personal struggles. The High Control, High D becomes highly stressed when he loses control to another person or has to deal with circumstances outside his control. *Controlling* expends a lot of energy that takes away from *doing*, and this is stressful for High D's.

PERSONAL EMPOWERMENT AND THE HIGH D

So how does the High D survive, thrive and keep from self-destructing? Following are a few suggestions to help you think differently and develop a personal action plan.

1. Re-think your level of personal expectations. You may need to lower your sights in terms of quantity of things you are trying to do.

2. While you lower the quantity bar, consider raising the quality bar where applicable. While it is true that High D's do a lot (quantity), sometimes the quality level is not what it could or should be.

3. Learn to give up control voluntarily. Recognize the added burden it places on you and the amount of energy lost trying to control things.

4. Absolutely, positively find the stress release that suits you best. Just make sure you find one. The stressed out High D's are the ones who want those fender-mounted, heat seeking missiles I mentioned earlier. A great stress release for the High D is physical activity or exercise; sweating. (This assumes overall health is good and your doctor approves.) It re-charges their batteries.

The High "I"

Let's move to the upper right hand quadrant and consider the influencer whom we'll call the High I for the sake of brevity. *Influence, inspire, impulsive, interactive* are four very accurate descriptors of the High I. While these people share the high energy level of their High D counterparts, their focus is very different. They answer the WHAT questions with people-related responses.

STRENGTHS

They are highly energized by being around and working with other people. And they HATE being alone! These high energy relaters are by nature good influencers and inspirers of others. They have a knack for looking for the good in people and are typically very optimistic. They are usually emotional people who tend to lead with their hearts. They tend to be very persuasive talkers and have a knack for convincing others to go along with their way of thinking.

You usually know how they *feel* about something whether you want to or not! The fact that High I's are highly interactive people is obvious by watching them "work a room." Whether it is an office party, dinner party, or sporting event, High I's have a strong need to be seen and to see all their *friends*. You need to understand that they define *friends* as anyone with whom they have ever met or come in contact.

Example. One of my highly interactive friends has season tickets to the Braves games and frequently talks about being at the baseball games with *Ted and Jane.* She means Ted Turner and Jane Fonda. Ted owns the Braves team. They sit behind the dug-out way down low in the best seats in the house. My friend is indeed "at the games" with them, however her tickets are in the nose bleed section of the uppermost deck. But to a High I, it doesn't matter. After all they were in the same stadium together, and she's sure she saw them in the parking lot after the game! High I's also have to go to the bathroom and concession stands a lot during such events. I guess you see more people there, too.

WEAKNESSES

Well if you haven't guessed by now, our High I friend's most troublesome problem is that they tend to talk too much. No, they don't tend to . . . they do talk too much. There is a saying that "generally speaking High I's are generally speaking!" Who would have thought that an innocent little greeting first thing in the morning like "how are you" could lead to a discussion that ends about lunch time? High D's have been known to get off elevators several floors early when riding up alone with a High I who is talking about her weekend.

A second interesting weakness is that High I's are generally disorganized. You go into their office and all you see are piles. You're sure there is a desk under there and a person behind it, but you couldn't swear to it. You hear a voice on the phone laughing and having a good time with whoever is on the other end. You assume it is an old friend or family member only to hear your talkative friend end the conversation by saying to the person on the other end "That's OK, sometimes I dial the wrong number too!"

Performance is less of an issue with the High I than their High D counterparts. The potential trap the High I falls into is the *approval trap.* Because their self-esteem is so tied to recognition by others, they perform in a sense for approval. They need this recognition and sometimes go to extremes to get it. I've noticed in my programs and workshops that they are always the first to volunteer if it means coming up on stage or even to the front of the room. I've also learned never to give the microphone to a High I because you might not get it back!

When this need for approval and recognition isn't met, feelings of failure and frustration may arise that can quickly surface the *blamer* in this person. As we said previously, the blamer wants someone else to be responsible for their problems.

PERSONAL EMPOWERMENT AND THE HIGH I
Following are a few suggestions for my High I friends that would help them understand personal empowerment, building on their strengths and developing their weaknesses.

1. Learn to value and seek out some "time alone" to rest and recharge your batteries. Alone is not a four letter word. Sometimes our inability to be alone is speaking to some personal insecurity. I don't want to get too psychological sounding here, but it is true.

2. Along the same lines, the stress release for High I's is talking it out. They need to "dump their buckets" to feel better and release stress. Make sure you have this outlet through friends or family so you won't have to hold High D's hostage in the elevator. It helps avoid going down the blaming path.

3. Personal recognition is great, and everyone wants to find approval in something. However, you must understand that your value as a person doesn't depend on always "winning awards" or this *recognition-based approval system* that can easily trap you. Recognize the intrinsic value you bring to the table through your incredible strengths as described above.

The High "S"
The words *supportive, steady, sympathetic* and *status quo* best describe those who most identify with the lower right hand quadrant. They

are people/relationally-oriented like the High I, but are slower and more deliberate in their approach to life.

STRENGTHS

High S's are the most supportive of the four styles. What do I mean by supportive? It is the very positive attribute of helping others. They are very patient and steady in their approach to life, taking things as they come. (This in contrast to the High D and High I who are pro-active and impulsive, respectively.) They are practical people who want to make sure they understand the HOW questions. High S's are the ones who usually write the manuals and procedures for HOW things work or businesses operate.

These *supporters* are "feelers" by nature. In other words, they rely to a great extent on how they feel about things (much like the High I). Because of this, they possess a great capacity for being sensitive to the needs and feelings of others. In today's corporate environment of high performance teams, the High S is the best team player and very loyal to the cause or company.

WEAKNESSES

The primary hurdle for the High S to overcome is their *resistance to change*. They dislike change immensely and do whatever it takes (up to the point of risking something) to maintain the *status quo*. You see examples of this resistance to change in all areas of their lives. Consider their daily routines. Once they get in one, you can't get them out of it. They drive to the office the same way each day and would not consider getting off the expressway at an earlier exit to save time in bad traffic. Sitting in traffic actually gives them a chance to read the paper, listen to their favorite radio talk show or simply visit with the others in their carpool . . . yes, these steady supporters actually carpool. There is one thing that not only disrupts their driving to work routine, but has also lead to panic attacks and other phobic disorders . . . the *detour* sign! If only they had known in advance, they could have called in sick until the construction ended.

Consider also the High S's toothbrush. Yuck. It is a disgusting old thing with the bristles all bent and curled over. It looks like something used to scrub the whitewalls on the tires instead of an instrument of oral hygiene. They get a new one each time they go to the dentist (every three to five years)! Perhaps the new toothbrushes recently on the market that have a color coded stripe that indicates it is time to get a new one when the stripe wears off will help them change!

The other personal style weakness facing the *supporter* is their indecisiveness and the corresponding slowness to act. Don't ever ask these people where they want to go for lunch. You will begin the long dialog process that sounds something like "I don't care, where do you want to go? Really, you decide", or the classic, "We *always* go to. . . ." They usually get to the ball park about the fifth inning because they couldn't decide who was going to drive and then where to park. "Gosh, do we park close so we don't have to walk very far, but then face the difficulty of getting out after the game, OR do we park far away so we can get out after the game, but have to walk a long way to the stadium carrying our stadium seats and coolers?" Life is filled with difficult choices.

At work, if their reports are late, it is because they couldn't decide which font looked best or if enough information was included. Sometimes the distribution list on these reports is longer than the report itself because they don't want anyone to feel left out. They can be overly sensitive to the "feelings" of others. Most of us could stand to *err* in this direction more often ourselves.

Like their High I counterparts, they can get caught in the *approval trap*. Theirs is different in that the trap comes more from *seeking acceptance* rather than recognition. Most of us like to feel accepted. Maslow describes it as a fundamental need. When the High S has unmet expectations and gets disappointed, she will often internalize it. This means too often they accept blame when it isn't hers to accept. Remember the *shamers* in Chapter 2? Here they come again if the High S doesn't realistically manage her need for acceptance.

Her stress release is very different from the D & I. Rather than the physical activity or emotional dumping, she needs time alone to deal with the stress. Believe it or not this often is in the form of *sleeping it off*. I have verified this with Gigi, my wife, who has many High S needs and this is one of them.

PERSONAL EMPOWERMENT AND THE HIGH S

Following are a few things to consider that may assist my High S friends in their personal empowerment efforts.

1. Practice in front of a mirror saying, "Change is inevitable, change is inevitable, change is inevitable." Once you've mastered this, then say "Change doesn't have to hurt (much)." No kidding friends, in our world today, change and God are the only remaining constants. (And even He uses change to make us grow!) So you might as well learn to accept it. Then you'll be surprised at how you can adapt and proactively manage it.

2. Nothing ever moves forward unless decisions are made and people take action. Neither will you. Your desire to gather information and try to please people is admirable. This grows out of your incredible strengths. BUT you must learn when enough is enough and move forward with decisions. You need to understand that people will respond in one of three ways: they will love your decision, they will hate your decision, or they won't care one way or the other. That's it. Making decisions doesn't have to hurt (much) either.

3. How you manage acceptance and rejection will go a long way toward determining your level of personal empowerment. Seeking the approval of those we love, respect, and work with or for is normal. We all want it. Our needs and motives for getting it are different, but we all want it. As a High S, you can go overboard seeking this approval. Try to maintain the balance between the pursuit and the trap.

The High "C"

The words *conscientious, cautious, careful* and *critical* best describe this fourth and final personal style. If your X ended up in the lower left hand quadrant, you will identify most with these tendencies and needs.

STRENGTHS

The High C is the most "thinking" of the four styles. She is very analytical by nature. She proceeds very cautiously in things, both personally and professionally. She is cautious in her decision making. Like her High S counterpart, she also gathers a lot of information before (or if) deciding. However there is a difference in motive. The High C gathers lots of information to carefully analyze it for accuracy and validity, while the High S primarily gathers it for support. High C's are very conscientious in their work. Quality, precision and accuracy are very important to them. This is particularly reflected in the quality of their work since they are so task/project-oriented. You could say they are the *quality control* people in our world. Based on their methodical approach to things, they are also good critical thinkers and problem solvers.

WEAKNESSES

As with the other three styles, the High C is not without personal challenges. Only, the word *challenge* is too strong for him. He doesn't like to be challenged at all and, in fact, is typically very *risk aversive*. He defines risk as doing something where you don't already know, or can't predict with high probability, what the outcome looks like. To the High C, risk is ordering the *flavor of the day* at TCBY instead of vanilla. When they get really excited and go hog wild, they ask for chocolate sprinkles on top. Whoa!

Their analytical and critical thinking skills serve them well in problem solving but get them in trouble on the personal side. They tend to get too critical of both themselves and others. (We'll deal with the latter later in the book.) The High C is his own worst critic. His perfectionist tendencies often cause his expectations to be way out of line (too high). No one can live up to them. Not himself, nor others. This is a lose-lose situation and often leads to disappointment.

Like his High S counterpart, the High C is slow in decision making and taking action. But again the reasons differ. Our cautious friend *fears being wrong* more than anything else. Thus he enters into what we call "paralysis of analysis." This fear also causes him to be too argumentative at times defending his position or opinion.

Also like the High S, our conscientious friend needs time alone to deal with stress. Rather than sleep it off, he needs time to think and reason things out. Since he tends to be a process thinker, he carefully considers how he got into this mess or tries to understand what went wrong.

PERSONAL EMPOWERMENT AND THE HIGH C

1. Learn to appreciate the fact that no progress was ever made where someone didn't take a risk of some sort to some extent. I'm not suggesting that you go "bungee-jumping." I am suggesting that you consider how being too risk aversive has or can limit you personally and professionally.

2. Your challenge is the opposite of your High D counterpart. Instead of *raising the bar*, you may need to consider *lowering the bar*. Don't misunderstand. I'm not suggesting you change your quality approach. I am suggesting that you can do away with the perfectionist tendencies by doing the *reality check* on your expectations as suggested earlier.

3. *Paralysis of analysis*. It is just what it says—*paralyzing*. The inability to move or act. For the High C, this is tied to the fear of being wrong; the need to be right. A good practice is to ask yourself a few questions. Is this decision life and death, important, routine, or a "no-brainer?" Can I make a reasonable decision based on the information available to me now? What are the consequences of being right? of being wrong? Learn to act/decide in what others consider a reasonable time frame. Ask someone else what they think (not another High C).

A Few Closing Thoughts On Personal Style Issues

I recall a few years ago discussing a program I had put together for a very large corporation. The person reviewing it informed me that they weren't interested in the parts that included using the personal styles profile instrument. I was told they had already used something like that years before. My response was "Great, how did it change your life and your business?"

I obviously believe strongly in the power that can be derived from tools such as these. If the answer to the above question was "It didn't," then I suggest you didn't get your money's worth. I hope this time around you have gotten your money's worth. I also hope you will begin now *applying* these principles you have learned. They can and will make a difference in your personal and professional lives. Let me close this chapter with a quote from one of our favorite authors and speakers, Zig Ziglar.

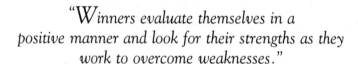

"Winners evaluate themselves in a positive manner and look for their strengths as they work to overcome weaknesses."

I hope you will use this material and begin to do this today.

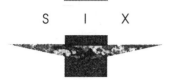

Understanding What Turns My Crank . . . Personal Empowerment and Motivation

"I will do what I want, when I want, because I want . . ."

Y ou may be wondering why no name appears below this quote. The main reason is there simply wasn't room to list all of our names there. You see, we've all said this on occasion. We've all thought it more often than we've said it. And we've done so throughout the course of our lives. It starts about one millisecond after we enter the world from our mother's womb and start breathing. (My wife suggests it starts within the womb as babies kick and squirm letting you know they didn't appreciate that Mexican food feast you consumed last night, re-fried beans and all!)

Most of us would say the quote also sounds pretty selfish, and to a certain extent, it is. But it is how we think and feel at times. We see the world through our own perspectives (remember the perception wheel in Chapter 2). We like to function in our own comfort zones when we can. We like to do what *we* like to do, and do so whenever we can. We like to do things in our own timing, and do so when we can. It is, after all, human nature. And it starts when we are babies and continues as we grow older.

Consider Zach, our one year old. Zach is highly motivated by two things: food and more food. It seems he would eat all the time if it were left up to him. Like other toddlers, he also attempts to set his own schedule through his demanding ways. When he wants to eat or simply get attention, he exercises primitive oral communication rites; he screams. Depending on our degree of "frazzledness," he sometimes wins. If we caved in too often, he would soon view that as a learned response and Gigi and I would be perceived much like Pavlov's dogs (his scream instead of the bell). Is Zach selfish? You bet he is. He is not yet *learned* in the art and skill of inter-personal relationships.

Next up is Gracie, our six year old. Gracie is highly motivated by anything that is chocolate. She, like her dad, is a borderline *chocoholic*. I guess we shouldn't have potty trained her using the old M&M reward system. It worked like a champ. The funniest thing about that experience was when her mom left the door open while going to the bathroom. Gracie went in to reward her with, you guessed it, M&Ms.

Our oldest is Trey, our eight year old son. He is easy going and fun-loving. With that said, we are still trying to figure out how to motivate him to do certain "unfun" things like clean up his room. Our threats seldom work. After four hours (my exaggeration) in the time-out chair, he tells me there are 4,250 squares in the dining room ceiling (he's real good in math).

Occasionally we send him to his room and instruct him not to come down until he has picked up his toys and cleaned up his room. A *couple of days later*, we think we ought to go up and check on him. There he is laying on his bed reading a book or playing with the things he was sent to pick up in the first place. Funny how he hadn't wanted to play with them for the week they had been in the middle of his floor. Time doesn't mean much to him at this point in his life.

Let's turn our attention to us grown up kids. Certainly we have more maturity and balance in our lives than our children. Surely we no longer look at things through our own paradigms of personal satisfaction and needs being met. Do we? Consider the following scenario at the office.

The smell of a new *initiative* is in the air. (The word *initiative* is one of those buzz words that some other consultant or academician thought up to avoid using the word program. You see some of the quality gurus deemed *program* a bad word that had to be replaced by the word *process*. Since many execs and especially the sales types didn't like the word *process*, they came up with the word *initiative*. How's that for *value-added*. There's no extra charge for that brief treatise on these trendy words.)

Back at the office, people are buzzing because the president of the company just got back from one of *those* seminars to teach him what they already know! Here we go again. This time we are going to re-engineer and facilitate pro-active positive change. Are we excited or what? Everyone is poised to embrace this newest *initiative* and implement it with even more zeal than the last three company-wide initiatives. Right?

Everyone, that is, except the operators out on the shop floor. They don't want another new way of doing the same old things. And, of course, there are the front office managers. They're still trying to figure out how *empowered* they really are. Can they sign for more copier paper without checking with the boss? Does purchasing need to approve this one?

So who does that leave? The field sales force. Oh yeah, those people out in the field somewhere. No, it couldn't be them. They haven't liked or cooperated with any new program we have done "on the inside." They think these programs exist to keep us out of our offices in meetings and away from their phone calls.

So who really is motivated by this newest program to save our jobs, our customers, our business and anything else worth saving? Jack, the president. As I said a few minutes ago, he just returned from a seminar sponsored by the "guru of the year." The scary part is he took lots of notes. He is really highly motivated about this stuff. He loves change (as long as he causes it). You simply need to "buy-in, get on board, own the process," etc., etc.

Does that scenario sound even vaguely familiar? This scenario fits many companies today to some extent. It brings to mind several questions related to motivation. Who gets excited and highly motivated by these new initiatives? How about you? What stirs you to action? What causes you to "buy-in and own" one thing and not another? In other words, what motivates you?

The answers lie in understanding personal empowerment and personal motivation. The balance of this chapter focuses on helping you better understand them.

PERSONAL EMPOWERMENT

Personal Operating Systems. Sounds like an engineer's approach to life, doesn't it? It really isn't. It is simply a way for me to tie together the three primary elements we discussed in the earlier chapters. These elements may be considered our *inner core* as individual people. Character . . . *who we really are.* Values . . . *why we do what we do.* Personal style (needs and behaviors) . . . *what we do and how we do it.*

You can see from the diagram in Figure 1, I added a central, focal point. I call it the *spiritual center.* Already some of you are saying to yourselves "Here we go, he's gonna start preaching or getting religious on us or give us some far out ethereal stuff." That is not my intention. The point I want to make is that *everyone has a spiritual center from which they operate.* Whether or not you consider yourself a *religious* or *spiritual* person, you have one. We all do. The spiritual center ties the other three together to keep them aligned and in balance. Consider it like the hub of a wheel with character, values, and style being the spokes. They are all necessary for the wheel to function. But without the hub tying the spokes together, they are much less effective and may even be rendered useless.

Blaise Pascal was a noted French mathematician, scientist and philosopher who lived in the seventeenth century. The computer language Pascal bears his name as does one of the measures of pressure, Pascals. (If he had died in a laboratory explosion, we could have said he went up in a *blaise of smoke.* Sorry, I couldn't resist.) Pascal made a very profound observation (as many philosophers do).

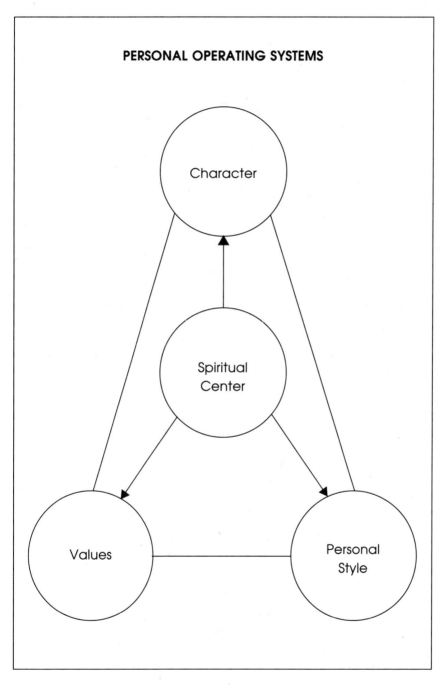

Figure 1

He said "Inside the heart of every person is a God-shaped vacuum that only He can fill."

Many people spend much of their lives attempting to fill this vacuum in various ways. Some fill it, as Pascal (and I) did, through a personal relationship with a personal God. Others fill it with themselves as they seek to be the best they can through self-maximization and personal happiness. Others use money, the stars, power or other people. But we all choose something. Why is this important? Why risk having some of you close the book again at this point? The reason is two-fold, like the book. The first is to bring you to a better understanding of what empowers and motivates you personally. Secondly, we want to examine how this impacts the inter-personal side of life (and we will do so in the second half of the book).

So let me leave this discussion of personal empowerment and personal operating systems with a couple of thoughts. Personal empowerment stems from the degree of alignment and congruence within our personal operating system. At the core of our personal operating system is our spiritual center. This spiritual center is the *driving force* in our lives. It is what compels and propels us forward. Now let's turn our attention to understanding *personal motivation*.

PERSONAL MOTIVATION

There probably aren't many subjects about which more has been said (through motivational speakers). There has been a lot less written perhaps because some view defining motivation like eating a bowl of soft gelatin with your fingers. It's hard to get a grip on it! Most of us are at least somewhat familiar with the early work of Abraham Maslow and his *hierarchy of needs* motivational theory. We may also be familiar with the later work of Frederick Herzberg. Herzberg applied motivational theory to the workplace to examine, among other things, worker productivity and motivation related to their environment.

The Personal Empowerment and Motivation Model© (see Figure 2) attempts to depict the relationship I want to establish between

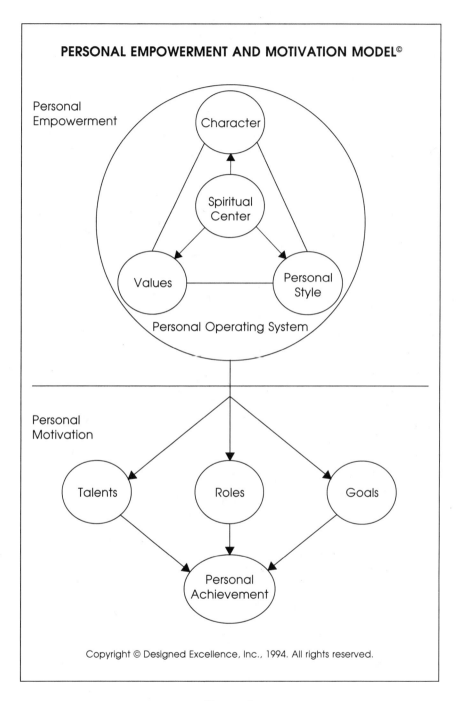

PERSONAL EMPOWERMENT AND MOTIVATION MODEL©

Personal Empowerment

Character

Spiritual Center

Values

Personal Style

Personal Operating System

Personal Motivation

Talents

Roles

Goals

Personal Achievement

Figure 2

personal empowerment and personal motivation. I suggest people move from being personally empowered to personally motivated.

Consider the following analogy. Gigi, my wife, makes some of our bread products from scratch. A couple of years ago, we invested a fair amount of money in the equipment to do so. She even mills the grains into flour. (I haven't shown that much interest yet, since she hasn't figured out how to make whole grain cupcakes and brownies.)

To make bread, you take several individual ingredients and mix them together. These include flour, water, and eggs. Once they are well blended, you knead it (physically abuse the lump until you beat it into submission). Then you bake it and it comes out of the oven as bread. (Gigi tells me this is a High D's version of the bread making process.)

While we have acknowledged that it is bread, I left out a key ingredient. It is the ingredient that turns it from ordinary (unleavened) bread into a beautiful, fully developed loaf of bread. The key is *yeast*! It causes the bread to *rise to the occasion* into, what most consider, a more useful or desirable form. Allow me to relate empowerment and motivation to the unleavened bread and the yeast.

Personal empowerment means that I have all the ingredients it takes to become the best I can. All the right stuff is there, yet I need something more to actually help get me there. This is motivation, or the motivating factors listed in the model in Figure 2. To maximize personal motivation and the opportunity for personal success and achievement, you must include: *talents*, *roles*, and *goals*.

These are the *catalysts* that, like yeast, facilitate the process to completion. My engineer and scientist friends will understand this analogy. *Catalysts* are agents that stimulate or precipitate a reaction, development or change. These motivating factors (talents, roles, and goals) are catalysts that help us move from simply understanding our personal operating systems to putting them into action. Personally we are motivated by our internal catalysts: talents, roles, and goals. Following are discussions of each and how they are integrally related to personal motivation and success.

Talents

The best and simplest way to define the word *talents* is: *what you are good at.* Pretty profound isn't it? No, it is just that simple. What are you good at? What are the things you do that cause people to recognize your talents, comment on how good you are at something, or encourage you to keep doing something?

Notice the involvement of others. I believe this is necessary to help us avoid the *legend in our own mind* syndrome some of us may fall prey to. There are certainly things that we may be good at that others don't know about; some hidden talent as it were. Don't discount those. But first consider those talents that others have identified with you, or agreed that you have talents in a particular area.

I have heard other advisors add another aspect to this discussion. It involves answering the question *what do you like to do?* Let me caution you on this one. Just because you like to do something, doesn't mean you're good or talented in that area. Anyone who has played golf with me can testify to that. I love to play golf. I wish I were really good at it. But alas, I am not. My expectations are way out of line (remember Chapter 3). I want to be good at it. I'd love to be considered a talented golfer, and on occasion I play pretty well, but at this point in my life I am only an average golfer.

Actually, compared to the other hackers out there, I'm a pretty good *average* golfer considering the time I spend at it. More than any other sport, golf is a time consuming one. It takes a lot of practice just to be average! It takes 5–6 hours (total time including travel and clubhouse) to get in a round in most places. On top of that, it is the hardest sport I've ever undertaken. Mark Twain said "Golf is a great way to ruin a walk." He obviously had at least attempted to play.

Talents typically are those "God-given" abilities for doing things that seem to come easy to us. They flow and don't seem much like work. It doesn't mean you don't work at them and develop them. You do. The key is discovering them. *Blessed is the person who knows what s/he is good at and gets to do it as a lifework.*

Some people are gifted athletically. Do they work at it? You bet! They work very hard if they want to perfect their gifts and compete at high levels. Others can't walk across a carpeted room without stubbing a toe once or twice. Others are mechanically inclined and good with their hands. Then there are those of us who go to the office Monday mornings wearing band-aids and ace bandages from our weekend of working around the house using various tools. For me it is sharp-bladed implements. I don't know why, but every time I use one, I bleed. Another real talent identifier is the person with a perpetually black and blue thumbnail. This person is a real wiener wielding a hammer. He intermittently hits the nail between blows to his thumb.

So I ask you again, what are you good at?

Roles

Now that we better understand talents, we need to discuss the role of *roles*. To help clarify what is meant by roles, we could examine a couple of scenarios. The first would be a sports team. Let's choose baseball. You probably know there are nine positions on a baseball team when it is on the field. In addition, in the dugout, there is a manager and several coaches. In the front office, there are executives including a general manager, team president, and eventually you get to an owner.

Let's examine first the players on the field. You could break it down into two categories: those who throw and those who field (catch) the baseball. All nine players do both. However the primary role of all the fielders, except one, is fielding. The pitcher is the one primarily responsible for throwing (pitching) the baseball. His job is pivotal. If he doesn't do it, there is no game. His role then is one of team leader. He is part of the team as a player, but has the lead role. The other players in the field play more of a support role in getting the players on the other team out.

Let's move to the dugout. The manager is often called the field general. He is responsible for putting the right players in the right positions on the field. He is responsible for game strategy; planning and implementation. He calls the shots on the field. The coaches are there to support the manager and players. They signal the manager's plans to the players during the game. Again we see the roles primarily as leader (manager) and supporter (coaches).

Now let's move upstairs to the executive offices. The owner/CEO sits in the stands and watches his/her team. They almost never have a say in the games or game plans (with the exception of Yankees owner George Steinbrenner, of course). The team president runs the operational aspects of the overall team franchise. This is the business side of the business. The general manager (when there is one) typically heads up all the baseball operations related to the team's major and minor league baseball operations, i.e. players, managers, coaches and related matters. Again, we see two types of roles; the CEO who is more aloof and removed from day to day operations, and the executives whose roles are to be involved more on a day to day basis.

The question is with which role do you most identify? Team player-supporter or team player-leader? Leader-manager or coach? CEO or operating executive? Hopefully you can identify with one or more of these. If not, perhaps you most identify with the vendor in the stands walking down the aisles yelling at the top of his lungs, "Cold beer here."

The second scenario involves individual sports. Golf, tennis, bowling, and those sports that predominantly involve individuals competing against each other or themselves. I know there are team events involving these sports, but usually they are individual in nature; my talent against yours. I win, you lose. With the predominance of teams in today's corporate environment, you may think discussing the individualist is a waste of time. Based on the fact that two of the four personal styles (discussed in Chapter 5) prefer to work alone in the first place, it isn't. (But that is a subject best discussed in another book.)

Some people's roles are best defined as *individualists*. If you think otherwise, simply consider the number of new businesses started each year, for the most part, by entrepreneurial individualists. The question you need to ask yourself is do you see your role as that of an *entrepreneurial individualist* or a *security-based individualist*? The latter prefers the security of the established organization. Both are individualists. Risk (or risk avoidance) is a determining factor.

Author's note: The whole concept of *role preference* was introduced to me a number of years ago by Bobb Biehl, a master consultant and friend. Bobb's wisdom and insights in this area stimulated my personal thinking a great deal. His consulting personally helped me sort out some of these issues in my own life. I am very grateful to him for this.

Goals

We've considered talents (what I'm good at) and roles (the position I want to play). The final power tool in personal motivation is *goals.* We'll define a goal much as the dictionary does, *an objective or purpose toward which one works.* Synonyms include *aim, intention,* and *purpose.* Many of us have been through a course on goal setting or read articles or books on the subject. The purpose of this discussion is to link goals to personal motivation.

The late J.C. Penney, a man of great character, said "Give me a stock clerk with a goal, and I will give you a man who will make history. Give me a man without a goal and I will give you a stock clerk." For goals to be a significant part of personal motivation, they must align with talents and roles as discussed above. In addition, goals must be realistic and owned by you.

You may recognize that this discussion of goals parallels somewhat the one on *expectations* in Chapter 2. Don't misunderstand. You don't have to be the one who sets them, but *you must own them.* In personal goal setting, hopefully you *control* the outcome as well. Don't set goals you neither own nor control.

Setting *realistic* goals is a matter of degree. They can and ought to be at both ends of the spectrum. Regarding setting lofty goals, Zig Ziglar says "Go as far as you can see and when you get there, you will always be able to see farther." There ought to be those goals that stretch us to the limit of our talents and roles. There also ought to be those that are slam dunks! No-brainers. Everyone needs successes. Everyone needs to win sometime. We need to learn to succeed.

A FINAL WORD ON PERSONAL EMPOWERMENT
AND MOTIVATION

Someone may ask why the Personal Motivation model doesn't end with *goals*. The reason is pretty simple. We can set goals as described above and never go after or achieve them. The distance between the *goals circle* in the model and the *achievement/success* one is what we call *hard work*. It takes action and work to accomplish our goals.

Remember, the word motivate comes from the same root word for *motion, motor* and *move*. It is the accomplishment of these goals that leads to achievement. It maintains alignment and congruence with our personal operating system. It is a cycle; a closed-loop process. Operating within it re-energizes us, helps maintain the balance we need, and keeps it fun in the process!

PART TWO

Connecting Tools— *Building Relationships with Others*

INTRODUCTION

C onnecting Tools. They do just what the name implies. They *connect* us with other people. And it doesn't have to hurt! It isn't like getting a shot in the old *gluteus maximus* or something. Connecting tools, when understood and used properly, build empowering relationships that endure.

The first part of this book discussed *forming tools* and the emphasis was on building you. This part is about *building other people* through successful relationships. We want to help build people who succeed. Successful people create and maintain successful businesses. It is a *paradigm shift* in the thinking of some to realize this is true. You can build a successful business by using people. Many hard charging entrepreneurs have done it over the years. But I submit you can't maintain one without building people who continue to build and maintain the business.

I also believe that we (all of us) have a responsibility to build into the lives of others as well; those with whom we work and co-exist in our society. Out of my personal paradigms of values and principles comes this belief. I believe that I will be held accountable for my part in building up my wife and children. I need to be a good steward of all that has been entrusted to my care, including these precious people. My desire is to see them become all that God wants them to be. That is one of the primary driving forces (and privileges) in my life.

Being human, we don't always succeed. Most of us would admit that we have at times experienced miserable failure in some relationships in the past. But we need to try, and keep on trying. Don't quit. *The only time you really fail is when you fail to try.* We must aim to succeed and to do so, we must keep working toward hitting the target. I hope these connecting tools help you build people who succeed in life. To settle for anything less would miss the mark.

S   E   V   E   N

Forgiving, Forgetting and Forging Ahead . . . Three Keys to Successfully Getting on with Your Life

"Forgetting what lies behind and reaching forward to what lies ahead, I press on toward the goal . . ."

THE APOSTLE PAUL

or many of us, the primary problem we face in our present relationships and the ones we will face in future relationships is past relationships. Many of us could work for the airlines as *baggage handlers* because we haul around so much of it everywhere we go. And that is the problem . . . *baggage*. Doesn't it irk you when the person you're sitting beside on the plane brings on all his "carry-on" baggage? You know it won't fit "neatly under the seat in front of him or in the overhead bin." The jerk! Why doesn't he check some of that stuff at the gate? Why must he constantly be getting up and down to get stuff out of these bags? Why doesn't he just leave some of that baggage behind? Does he really need all that stuff?

We all bring a suitcase or two with us to relationships; at least a "carry-on"-sized bag. Some of us bring trunks! While I don't want to spend a lot of time on the sources of this baggage, it is important to understand where it comes from. (I know you're not supposed to end a sentence with a preposition, but this sounds a lot better than saying "from whence it cometh.")

It is really pretty simple. Baggage comes from *people* and *experience*; experience with people; mostly bad experiences with people. In other words, failed relationships. And not necessarily your own. We are all aware of (or perhaps have heard) some of the unfortunate statistics involving those from broken homes and families. The probability of similar things occurring in the lives of those coming from such backgrounds is higher than those from healthy ones. For example, the probability of someone becoming an alcoholic is higher for those coming from a home where someone is an alcoholic.

Perhaps you have been fortunate enough that you have not experienced such difficulties personally. However, it has been my experience and observation that we have all experienced *fractured* relationships at some point in time, both personally and professionally. The purpose of this chapter is not to dwell on the causes, but to provide tools for re-building and repairing the damage to the present ones and prevent (or minimize) it in future ones.

The key to harnessing the power in these tools comes from understanding and applying the three F's: *forgiving, forgetting,* and *forging ahead.*

FORGIVING

The dictionary defines forgiving as *granting pardon; ceasing to blame.* This is the core principle of the Christian faith. It is also a major tenet of most of the world's other major religions. Regardless of the "spiritual center" from which you operate, it remains a critical factor in building and maintaining successful relationships. And it starts with you and me.

Many of us have *internalized* our baggage to such an extent that we always blame the same person when things go awry . . . ourselves. Some take the other extreme, *externalizing* their problems and always blame someone else. We need to grant pardon; cease to blame in both cases. Why? Our health depends on it: physical, emotional and spiritual.

We all know people (or at least have read about those) who literally make themselves sick worrying, blaming, holding grudges, and resenting other people. The physical manifestations can be devastating: headaches, some severe illness and diseases, sexual disorders, etc. The emotional disorders can also be dramatic leading to medication and even hospitalization.

"To err is human, to forgive divine." Susan had gone through a very bad divorce. She was stressed out. Her stress release was shopping for antiques. She loved to go out and browse through the antique stores to calm her nerves. One day while doing so, she came across an old brass lamp that caught her attention, so she bought it. When she got home, she immediately got out the brass cleaner and began to polish it, rubbing off the tarnish.

Much to her surprise (not yours, I'm sure), out popped a genie! The genie offered her the standard three wishes. But there was one caveat. Everything she wished for, her ex-husband got twice as much. She didn't care much for this exception, but agreed to it. Her first wish was for a million dollars. She never had enough money to really make ends meet so she wanted financial security. The genie granted her wish informing her that if she called her bank she would find her balance to be a million dollars plus the $36.78 she already had. AND her ex-husband got two million put into his account. This sort of steamed her, but no matter . . . on to her second wish.

For her second wish, she decided on a string of real pearls. Her "ex" was such a tightwad and never bought her anything nice, so she wanted to get something nice for herself. Again the genie granted her wish informing her that when she opened her jewelry box, she would find a beautiful strand of pearls. BUT her ex-husband got two strands, and he gave them to the women he had been running around with. This really steamed her. It was too much to take.

The genie prodded her for her third wish. She thought long and hard on this last one. Finally she burst into laughter. She became nearly hysterical. The genie asked what could possibly be so funny. Susan told him, "Genie, I've decided what I want for my third wish. I want you to scare me half to death!"

While this story always draws a lot of laughter from audiences when I tell it, it also typifies how some of us feel on occasion. We think more about getting even than forgiving. Revenge can be a strong motivator.

The inability to forgive is one of the primary killers of relationships. Relationships cease to exist when *unforgiveness* exists between two people. How tragic it is to see a family torn apart because a husband or wife can't forgive his or her spouse for something. As parents, we often end up teaching these things to our children; usually unintentionally. How sad it is to see young people harboring so much anger and bitterness toward their parent(s). They start by blaming their parents for all their problems and dysfunctions. Then they carry the baggage into their personal and interpersonal relationships. This baggage is too heavy to carry, even for most mature adults. It is virtually impossible for young people to carry that much of a load, so they dump it on others. Why would anyone want to bring that kind of negative baggage into a marriage or family relationship? As was alluded to previously, failed relationships can proliferate failed relationships and so on and so on . . .

Consider our interpersonal relationships with people at work. John and Gloria are both department managers for the same company. He is in charge of marketing, and she has the sales responsibility. They report to the same vice-president. Both are members of the same cross-functional management team. As is typical of these two functions, they don't always see things from the same perspective. Different perspectives are okay, even healthy at times, but not here. They have developed a growing resentment of each other and often see their functions as competitive instead of cooperative.

John thinks Gloria got her promotion because she is female and African-American. He also thinks she "strongly dislikes and resents men." Gloria thinks John got his MBA from "Suck-up" University and learned to say "I agree with whatever you think" in eight different languages. He always seems to be touting his own accomplishments in front of the team and their boss, looking for pats on the back.

A little background information will bring some perspective to this situation. Gloria had a difficult childhood. Her dad walked out on their family when she was young, causing tremendous stress on her mom. She had to work two jobs and thus had little time for Gloria and her brothers and sisters. Gloria, being the oldest, had to spend a lot of her time "helping" with the younger children. She has strong negative feelings about her father whom she refuses to talk about. She has a difficult time in personal relationships with "men" friends.

John comes from a very different background. His family had money so John always had everything he wanted. The problem is he didn't have *what he needed*: his dad's *acceptance*. John's dad was a very stern man with a critical spirit. No matter what John did, he could never please his father. He did all that he knew to do as a child to please his dad, but it was never enough. As far back as he can remember, his dad was always correcting him or letting him know that what he did could always be a little better. It was never enough. If he made the team, his dad wanted to know why he didn't make first string, and so on . . .

Back to John and Gloria at work. Do they bring this baggage to the office? Absolutely. Do they have to? Absolutely not. Get ready to underline or highlight this next line because it is worthy of your best yellow highlighter. Forgiveness is a CHOICE. Bitterness, anger, resentment and holding grudges are CHOICES. The best thing about this is that it is YOUR choice. Finally, there is something in life that is absolutely, positively your choice. Remember the chapter on expectations? Realistic, Control, Ownership. When it comes to (personal and interpersonal) forgiveness, you have control; you own your feelings. So what do you choose?

There is an irony that exists here as well. When you choose not to forgive, the person involved maintains control. They continue to *win* in a sense. When we choose not to forgive, the overbearing or abusive parent, the unfaithful "ex-", the jerk you used to work for, all continue to exercise a sort of control over you. We need to take back control of the situation and re-own our feelings. Allow me to leave the subject of forgiveness with the following. *With forgiveness comes freedom; without it you are in bondage. And the choice is yours.*

FORGETTING

Forget: to be unable to remember something. While forgiving is the power tool that re-builds relationships, *forgetting* allows them to grow and flourish again. Another paradox exists here. Most of us have the capacity to forget all kinds of things we *want to remember*; and even greater capacity to remember the things *we want to forget*. Why? I don't know and if I did I'd be writing another book about it. Here's what I do know. The ability to forget after forgiving is a tremendous gift.

How many of us have gone through situations where we screwed up, worked through the forgiveness process and thought the relationship was restored only to be reminded of what we did, in a future confrontation? We love that don't we? Our children particularly love it. "Thanks, dad, for reminding me of that thing I did that you said was forgiven and forgotten. I really appreciate you bringing it up again. I had almost forgotten it myself. Thanks for the little reminder."

It is also a real marriage builder. For the newlywed it sounds something like this, "Thanks, honey, for reminding me again that I don't cook or keep the house like your mom did. Remind me one more time and we can make arrangements for her to do it for you, again!" And for those of us veterans of marriage, it sounds like this. "Thanks, dear, for reminding me that sometimes my temper gets the better of me. I would have sworn that paint can I kicked was empty," I said, as I sat in my easy chair with my foot elevated and my big toe in a cast!

In this context, forgetting is a powerful tool. It implies not dwelling in the past, digging up the past, or holding up the past (to others). The ability to forget allows you to start afresh with a relationship. It is a very empowering and endearing aptitude.

A young woman gave birth to her first child. Because her husband was away on military duty, she spent the first couple of weeks after the birth at her parent's home. One day she commented to her mother how surprised she was that the baby had dark hair since she and her husband were both blonde. Her mother reminded her that her father's hair was also dark. The young woman said, "Mom, that doesn't make any

*difference because you and dad adopted me." With a smile on her face,
her mother replied, "Oh yes, I always forget."*

Forgiving brings freedom and re-builds relationships. Forgetting allows relationships to flourish, grow, and restores peace of mind.

FORGING AHEAD

This one isn't very complicated. It simply means what it says. Forge
ahead. As the verse at the beginning of the chapter says, press on
toward the goal. You see, *unforgiveness drains our energy* so that we
are unable to pursue the goals we have set. We are sometimes unable to function. It can disable us partially or completely. We need
to preserve our energy to pursue our goals and do the things required
of us to get there. The inability to forget (or choosing not to) *dis-
tracts* us from our goals. There are many distractions in our lives. We
don't need to add to the list.

The expression *forging ahead* brings to mind an analogy Christ
used with his followers when he encouraged them to *"keep your hands
to the plow and do not look back."* If we take our hands off the plow,
the ox or mule takes control and heads off where it chooses. We lose
control.

If we look back, two things may happen. The first is we plow a
crooked furrough. We waste time and energy plowing land we didn't
intend to plow. The second thing that can happen is that when we
don't watch where we're going, we may step in ox poop! What could
be more distracting and time wasting than to have to stop and clean
that smelly stuff off our feet?

There's a lot of *ox poop* laying around for us to step in. The key
to avoiding it is to keep our eyes focused straight ahead (even if it
means you have to look at a lot of oxen posteriors or people who
act like them along the way), and press on toward the goal. Successful people are able to *forgive, forget* and *forge ahead* toward the goals
they have set for themselves. If they consider these past experiences
at all, it is simply to look at them as learning experiences and move
on. Walking through life's airports is a lot easier when you aren't
carrying a lot of excess baggage.

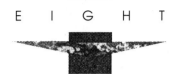

Building on a Solid Foundation . . . Respect, Trust, Integrity and Commitment

"Respect, huh!, I tell ya, I don't get no respect!"

RODNEY DANGERFIELD

R-E-S-P-E-C-T

Who among us hasn't roared with laughter listening to one of Dangerfield's self-depricating routines involving respect (or the lack of it)? I love the one in which Rodney says, "The other day my dog walks to the front door and starts barking like crazy. I go over to the door and open it. The dog didn't want to go out; he wanted me to leave." He gives us a very comical perspective on the whole issue of respect.

I want to introduce to you a building block approach for building solid relationships. It can significantly affect your marital, parental, leader-follower, and team member relationships. *The first tool is respect.* Like many of you, I was a great Motown music fan in the 60s and 70s. You probably remember one of the great classics with that sound was Aretha Franklin's RESPECT. *"What you want, baby I got it. What you need, you know I got it. All I'm asking is that you show me a little respect. R-E-S-P-E-C-T, find out what it means to me."* (You'll have to excuse me. I was the lead singer in a rock 'n roll band in High School, and I still get carried away at times with strong upbeat songs. My kids think their dad has lost it on occasion when I hear one and crank up the radio.)

Webster defines *respect* as *treat with consideration; value.* This meaning implies several things. The first is that I consider the thoughts and feelings of others with whom I want to establish a relationship. If we remember the principle, *different people may see the same thing differently,* can we still respect the person with whom we see things differently? This is one of the fundamental issues in conflict resolution (which is another discussion better left to another time). We need to ask ourselves this question, "Do my words and actions toward others demonstrate the courtesy and consideration due them as fellow human beings?" This leads to the second, and most important, part of the definition, *value.*

We talk a lot about *value* today in terms of quality, product and customer service. We even use it at times in the context of people. Many organizations today have values' statements that say something like "our people are our most valuable asset." This sounds terrific, BUT . . . in some organizations, there exists a considerable *gap* between the walk and the talk with this stated value. (I'll deal with this in more detail in just a minute.)

To value someone is to believe they have *intrinsic worth* as a human being. This has two facets. The first is personal. In a sense, I am revisiting the first part of the book. But it is extremely important to at least touch on the issue of self-respect. The value or intrinsic worth of you as a person. Perhaps you've seen the poster or cards that show a little child with the caption, "God don't make no junk!" Well, it's right, He don't! Maintaining a healthy self-respect is critical to creating and maintaining healthy relationships of any kind. People who have little or no self-respect don't do well in relationships; business or personal.

From an interpersonal perspective, value has an outward expression. We value others in that we believe they have a right to coexist with the rest of us and bring some value to the table in terms of potential or contribution. For example, someone new is hired in your department. You didn't have a say in hiring him, but you'll have to work with him. He has a degree in a field related to your work, and it is from a reputable school. Your department can certainly use some help as you are swamped with work. You think this new person will be able to help. So you have an initial respect for this person based on the above.

We've all heard of the MDR as it relates to vitamins and nutrition. Respect is the MRR (minimum relationship requirement). Respect is the cornerstone for any relationship. Without it, relationships can't exist at any level . . . not even superficially. Respect is an attitude. It is the attitude we have toward others. This attitude somewhat dictates what I think and feel about, and how I respond toward other people.

I was flipping through the channels on TV last night (my wife says I am a confirmed channel surfer). I came across an old "Taxi" rerun and caught this much of a conversation between Louie (Danny DeVito) and Alex (Judd Hirsch). Louie was trying to convince Alex to come with him to meet his girlfriend's parents as they were "nice people," and Louie didn't know how to act around nice people. He was trying to play on his "relationship" with Alex (the nice guy "cabbie" in the show). The conversation went something like this:

Louie: C'mon, Alex, do it for me as a friend.

Alex: Louie, we are not friends!

Louie: OK, then do it based on our past relationship and what we mean to each other.

Alex: We don't have a relationship, and we mean nothing to each other.

Louie: Then what do you call what we have here after all these years?

Alex: (after pausing to consider the question) What we have is a situation where two people exist, know the other one exists, and don't like each other.

I thought to myself what a great comical illustration for the discussion of respect (lack of) and relationships.

Finally, *respect is something we give to others*. It can't be demanded or taken. It is proactive on our part toward other people. As I said

before, it is based on the fundamental belief that a person has intrinsic value and worth. In the *Declaration of Independence*, Thomas
Jefferson wrote, "We hold these Truths to be self-evident, that all
men are created equal, that they are endowed by their creator with
certain unalienable rights, that among these are life, liberty and the
pursuit of happiness . . ." Perhaps no one has ever said it better than
Jefferson. So let's conclude by saying that *mutual respect* is the foundation upon which any relationship is built.

TRUST

The dictionary defines trust as *believe in; place confidence in*. This is
a BIGGIE! From our marriages to our companies, trust is a big issue. No, it is a huge issue. Most of us want to create and maintain
trust-based relationships. Most of us enter marriage believing we can
trust our mate. We want to be able to trust our children; particularly as they get older and exercise more freedom. We want to trust
the organization that employs us, the person we work for and the
people with whom we work. And yet . . .

Infidelity (extra-marital affairs) in marriages continues to grow. A
trust is broken. Children (especially teenagers) run away from relationships at home and/or turn to other people and sources of support (drugs and alcohol). The *trust gap*, often referred to as the *generation gap*, continues to be perpetuated. On the corporate side, the
old mantra of *a job for life* has been replaced in recent years with the
most massive loss of jobs since the Great Depression. And yet some
corporate executives wonder why there are trust and credibility issues causing severe problems at work.

Much of my internal consulting work is in the areas of creating
and helping organizations implement leadership, empowerment and
team-based initiatives. There are a couple of common threads in
each. One of the most important is trust: establishing or restoring
it. And it can be the most difficult assignment.

Now that we've established the need and looked at some of the
discouraging results of (a lack of) trust, what are some of the answers

to these challenging problems? Let's begin to address them by examining some basics of *trust*. The key element in creating and maintaining trust-based relationships involves only three words, and yet, is as difficult for some as spelling *supercalifragilisticexpialidocious*. (Remember *Mary Poppins*.) The three words are *rely on others*.

Trust requires that you learn to rely on others. It means that in some things I am willing to *give up control*. You will recall (from the chapter on personal style issues) that this is a huge issue for High D's. And our High C friends, being somewhat suspicious by nature, don't do it easily either. "Oversimplified," you say. Not, I reply. Think for a minute about a good trust-based relationship you currently enjoy.

Just to know someone is not to trust them. This could be no more than a "respect-based" superficial relationship. Just to work in the same building or department with someone doesn't imply trust. Trust only becomes a requirement when you have to work *with* someone and part of the desired end result requires that you rely on them. This begins the process of building (or not building) trust. Trust must be *earned* from people, and you must earn it from them.

Whether your situation involves building trust in your personal life or your team at work, I think the following quote from Emerson says it well. He wrote these words over 150 years ago. They describe how we should approach people and relationships, both personal and professional.

"Trust men and they will be true to you; treat them greatly, and they will show themselves great."

Following is an acrostic that provides some "how to's" required to build and maintain trust-based relationships.

T—reat other people the way you want to be treated (the Golden Rule principle).

R—ely on their word as truthful and assume the best until proven otherwise.

U—nderstanding: the other person's agenda, personal style and needs, values, etc.

S—upport in good times and bad.

T—ime: It takes time to create, build, and maintain empowering relationships. There are no short-cuts.

If you will accept my previous analogy that respect is the foundation upon which you build relationships, then trust represents the materials with which you construct them; the bricks and lumber that go into their construction.

INTEGRITY

One of the definitions that best suits the way I want to position the word *integrity* in this discussion is: *soundness, completeness, the quality or condition of being undivided.* Following is an excerpt from the discussion of integrity in the first chapter (Character).

> I like to describe it (integrity) as beliefs in action *and congruence between beliefs and behaviors. Integrity is not something held inside a person. It is not an internal quality. Rather it is an external one that is demonstrated to others through our actions.*

How do we relate integrity to relationships? The two key phrases are *beliefs in action* and *demonstrated to others through our actions*. The key word is *action(s)*. At this point, we assume the respect and trust are there. To hold the trust, we want to demonstrate integrity through our actions. It is the old *walk the talk* stuff we hear all the time, but don't necessarily see. We demonstrate our integrity by holding up our end of the bargain; following through on what we said we would do.

To carry the building analogy another step further, integrity represents the *mortar and nails* that hold relationships together. When the integrity of a relationship is compromised, it is difficult to hold it together.

Consider the following example. I said I would take the kids to see *Lion King* upon its recent strategic return to the theaters (just in time for the holidays—those Disney folks are savvy.) However, a couple of unanticipated year end programs were booked, and I was swamped preparing for them. I forgot about the movie commitment and put them off when reminded of it.

Gracie, our six year old with a tenacious memory and a paradigm of strict adherence to rules, asked me a question that got my attention. "Daddy, why is it OK for grown-ups to tell stories, but kids get in trouble for it?" Stunned, I told her it isn't like that; grown-ups aren't supposed to tell stories either. Then she nailed me. "So why didn't you take us to see *Lion King* like you promised?" Well, *Lion King* was pretty good, but I still liked *Beauty and the Beast* better.

While this may seem a simple story that really isn't that big of a deal, it is a huge deal. If we want our children's trust and to teach them integrity in relationships, we must earn the trust and maintain it through our integrity. Like most parents, I will do all I can to protect the integrity of those prized relationships with my family. If we fail to do so, the consequences can be severe, particularly as they get to the teen years. And isn't it interesting how kids who have terrible memories about picking up their rooms or getting home on time, have elephant-like memories when it comes to our promises (or what they think was promised).

In Gracie's mind, it really wasn't a trust issue, but an integrity one. The soundness of her relationship with her daddy (me) may have been shaken; maybe just a little. As busy parents we might be tempted to say it is not integrity but just the result of circumstances outside our control. And that's partially true. But that isn't the way she sees it. Remember we said *perception is reality*. I may even get away with it several times because children are so loving, trusting, and forgiving, BUT time will tell, and then it happens. Once the relationship's integrity is compromised (in the mind of either person), the next thing to crumble is the trust, and ultimately the respect. And then we have no relationship at all.

Back in the office, Martha is part of a high performance self-managed work team. The team has been in existence for two years and has functioned well. Martha is a pretty good team player, but still highly motivated by personal recognition (a High I personal style). On a couple of occasions she has taken personal credit for things that really were team accomplishments. This has caused problems from time to time with some of the other team members.

Another style related issue for the High I is that they tend to be disorganized. Martha is indeed disorganized. She typically is late for team meetings and at times doesn't have her team assignments together when they need them. The team has been pretty understanding, but their patience is wearing thin. They are beginning to wonder how to deal with Martha and dread the thought of team discipline. (Even high performing SMT's dislike the peer discipline part and often avoid it.)

Management has asked their team for a presentation to review their results and progress. They want to determine if they should continue to pursue the team approach to doing business or go back to more traditional means. This is the team's opportunity to shine. Each member is assigned a part of the management presentation. The team meets to review it in advance. Martha "isn't quite finished with her part yet", but assures the team she will be ready. When the big day comes, Martha not only isn't ready, she calls in sick that day and doesn't show up at all. The team has to go on anyway, as management presentations don't wait.

There is a big hole in their presentation, and they aren't sure what to do about it. They *are* finally sure what to do about Martha. It has now become an integrity issue and moving quickly toward a trust issue as well. Team discipline is in order. After looking somewhat unprepared for the management presentation, they wonder if *capital punishment* is one of their options! There is an old proverb that says, "A man who walks in his integrity, walks securely. One who perverts his way, will be found out." In the words of the Cowardly Lion in *The Wizard of Oz*, "Ain't it the truth!"

COMMITMENT

If *respect* is the foundation, *trust* the bricks and lumber, *integrity* the mortar and nails, then what could possibly be left in this building analogy? One last thing. *Commitment*. Webster defines commitment as *ownership; devotion to*. This is the final component. It represents the *maintenance* aspect. It keeps the construction materials intact over the long haul. If you have ever built a home (or had one built), you know what an incredible challenge maintenance can be.

Many of us love new things, especially houses. But unless the home is maintained over the years, some or all of the following will occur: the paint cracks and peels, boards rot, bricks get dirty and the mortar can dry and crack, floor boards creek and moan, nails may back out, roofs leak, basements leak, houses settle and walls can crack, doors stick, etc., etc. I think you get the picture.

Relationships need maintenance, too. If they don't get it, over time they (the people in them) may crack and split, get warped and out of balance, and settle, causing boredom and apathy. Like old doors and windows, people get stuck. They may slowly begin to leak. Integrity and trust are compromised, and finally the worst happens: warm, vibrant homes turn back into run down, empty houses.

Similar things happen at work. From the overbearing, dominant manager to the change resistant, non-confrontational one, over time, the same types of foundational cracks appear. Departments and morale crumble. The dominant manager tries to hold it together through force and power. The low assertive manager attempts to please everyone and ends up pleasing no one.

What does it take to *prevent* your relationships from getting to this stage or going down the wrong path. *Commitment*. People who are committed to relationships take *ownership* of the process. We are more committed to something we own. This is especially true of relationships.

When I own something, I usually take better care of it. Think about the cars you have rented. I dare say you have done (or considered) things in a rental car that you would not do with your own. Driving over curbs and medians because you missed your turn or exit, leaving the empty McDonald's coffee cups and leftover french fries on the floor, and driving over speed bumps in the parking lot at 55 mph are just a few. It gets worse if you've ever rented a house or apartment to someone. You find that people tend to care less for that which they don't own.

Another thing that people committed to a relationship do is accept responsibility for their attitudes and behaviors. We recognize that, while we do not control all aspects of the relationship, we do control our own attitudes and our behavior toward others. We commit to thinking and behaving in ways that seek the best for all concerned; not just ourselves. The latter refers to selfishness; plain old, "I'll take my ball and go home," or "Do it my way or I quit" selfishness. I am convinced that basic selfishness is the root of many, if not most, relationship problems. People who desire to build win/win relationships (as they are often called today), are committed to *unselfishness*; in themselves and others. We control the first person (us). We can only influence the second.

Finally, commitment is about success in relationships. Not many people go into relationships expecting or desiring to fail. Players on a team enter a competition expecting to win; not just expecting to play the game. If you simply show up to play, you won't necessarily give it your best effort. You will find that people who are *committed to the mutual success* of a relationship (whether a marriage or a work team), win far more often than they lose.

N I N E

Personal Style Elasticity . . . It May "Stretch You Out"
(Tools for Maintaining Successful Relationships)

"Do good to thy friend to keep him; to thy enemy to gain him."
BEN FRANKLIN

A young man was in the process of being interviewed for acceptance to morticians' school. During the interview, he was asked *why* he wanted to become a mortician. He replied, "You know, I've always liked working with people." While this isn't exactly the kind of "working with people" I had in mind for this chapter, it is a start for talking about how we *maintain relationships* with people over time.

Elasticity is an engineering term that relates to one of the key mechanical properties of materials. The easiest way I know to explain it for the non-technical person is in terms of *rigidity* and *resiliency*. A metal rod is more *rigid* than a plastic one of the same thickness or size. It takes more force to *bend* or *flex* steel than it does aluminum.

Take a paper clip and try to bend it. It is pretty easy to bend, primarily because of its small diameter. Now bend a coat hanger. The same is basically true, but it is a little more difficult. Now try to bend a High Speed steel drill bit that looks to be the same diameter as the coat hanger. Why can't you bend it? (or why not as easily?) The answer lies in its *modulus of elasticity*. Laymen's interpretation: it is more rigid; or *it isn't as flexible*.

Now let's consider the other aspect of elasticity: *resiliency*. Resiliency is the ability of something to bounce back. Consider the rubber band. Take one in your hand and stretch it. When you release it, it returns to its original shape. It is a highly elastic material.

The resiliency of the rubber band has provided many forms of entertainment and pain over the years. For young boys, one of the *rites of passage* was learning to shoot them across the room without getting caught. Another was learning to snap them on the behinds of others without getting slapped or beaten up. It seemed fun and funny at the time. (So, it is obvious we were starved for entertainment in my home town.)

Now take a piece of taffy. Stretch it out. Let it go to see if it snaps back. It doesn't. Why? Because it has such a low *modulus of elasticity* that it deforms very quickly and won't return to its original shape. It isn't very elastic and has no resiliency.

Another rite of passage for teenage boys was trying to break the plastic rings that come around six packs of canned beverages. The more you could fold and break at one time, the more *machismo* you demonstrated. If you could fold them all together so that you could break all six at once, you were super cool and macho. Whether you pulled one or all six together, *the plastic stretched* until it broke or your hands hurt so bad you had to quit. (Truth be known, this exercise hurt like crazy and often ended up with painful deep impressions in the sides of your hands and fingers. I also don't ever remember getting more dates or losing any because I could or couldn't break them.) In the end, either the plastic gave in or you did. It was truly a win-lose deal.

What is the purpose of this "engineering" lesson on material properties? People also have varying degrees of *rigidity* and *resiliency*. I believe these contribute to successful *maintenance* of relationships. I refer to this power tool as *personal style elasticity*. In the balance of this chapter we will examine the "what" and "how" of style elasticity. And I promise, no more engineering *stuff*.

There are a number of critical success factors that determine your degree of personal style elasticity. These factors include *willingness* and *ability, personal style considerations, teachability* and *maturity*. First let's consider *willingness* and *ability* individually, and then the various combinations of them. Then we'll re-visit *personal styles* to examine *what* needs to be stretched, and *how* it can be done.

The best definition I've read for *willingness* in this application is *eagerly compliant; done voluntarily*. Willingness is an *attitude*. And everybody has one. They range from very positive to very negative and everywhere in-between. Attitude is one of the most (and some consider it *the* most) important factors in determining success in relationships; perhaps even success in life. Consider the words of my favorite author and friend, Chuck Swindoll.

> "*The longer I live, the more I realize the impact of attitude on life. Attitude, to me, is more important than facts. It is more important than the past, than education, than money, than circumstances, than failures, than successes, than what other people think or say or do. It is more important than appearance, giftedness or skill. It will make or break a company . . . a home. The remarkable thing is we have a choice every day regarding the attitude we will embrace for that day. We cannot change our past . . . we cannot change the fact that people will act in a certain way. We cannot change the inevitable. The only thing we can do is play on the one string we have, and that is our attitude . . . I am convinced that life is 10% what happens to me and 90% how I react to it. As so it is with you . . . we are in charge of our attitudes.*"

Consider also these oft heard phrases. *I am willing to go the extra mile. I am willing to meet you half-way. I'm willing if you are.* They imply volunteerism on the part of the person who says them. It is interesting to note that when we refer to someone as "having an attitude," it means a negative or bad one.

The tandem critical success factor that goes along with willingness is *ability*. Ability is defined as a *natural* or *acquired talent*. It is a *skill* factor. As the definition implies, one person seems to come by it naturally, while another must acquire it. The best thing about ability is that, in most cases, it can be taught or transferred to another person. We all have the innate ability to learn, albeit in varying degrees.

In our personal and professional lives, our abilities (talents) either move us ahead, or the lack of them may hold us back. This is particularly true as it applies to our relationships. We don't often think of *willingness* and *ability* when it comes to just getting along with people or even developing close inter-personal relationships. We need to. Understanding how they may affect both is very important to our success. Let's consider four different combinations of these critical success factors.

HIGH WILLING/LOW ABILITY

This person has the right attitude. They simply don't possess the ability to cultivate and maintain strong positive relationships. Consider Kathy. She is a very capable person who wants to get into management. She has the technical tools necessary to do her job and carries out her assignments very well. She has advancement potential. However, she is a little weak on the inter-personal side in terms of working with others in a team dynamic.

During her recent performance review, her manager points this out to her in a responsible and constructive manner. Kathy's response? She asks how she can get the tools she needs to improve in this area. She recognizes it as one that needs development and wants to work on it. Kathy is very willing; she simply lacks the ability in this particular area. BUT she is teachable. She is willing to learn. She has a great attitude! Through education and training, she can develop the necessary skills to enhance her career and personal relationships.

LOW WILLINGNESS/HIGH ABILITY

Ralph's challenges are just about 180° from Kathy's. He has been through many of the company's programs on developing inter-personal relationships and leading-managing other people. He has also attended outside seminars in these areas as well as having considerable on the job management experience. Others in the organization perceive that he has all the talent or skill necessary. It seems to them like *he has an attitude*. He isn't willing to bend or flex. He is rigid in his approach to and dealings with people. (Except his boss, of course. He is politically astute enough to *schmooze* his way through when he has to.)

Ralph is perceived as arrogant by his peers. How do you deal with the Ralphs of your organization? The answer lies in the simplest management principle ever recorded. This is worth the price of the book. Many of us first learn this principle when learning to handle/ manage/discipline our young children. It is (music, please) . . . *you make the rewards/punishments feel so good or hurt so bad.* You want to change behavior? Create circumstances or outcomes that hurt so bad or feel so good, and you will be able to change behavior.

People with an attitude need an attitude adjustment. People like Ralph can wreak havoc on an organization. They are bad for morale. The decision NOT to deal with them sends a powerful (negative) message through your organization. Style elasticity tools can be taught and transferred to other people, but they must be *willing*.

Low Willing/Low Ability

This person usually represents a bad hiring decision. She was probably related to the owner or one of the key managers or worked her way through an inept hiring/interviewing process. Since this person represents the worst of both, she presents the greatest challenge to both fellow team members or managers. Here, I recommend *the three R's process*. Again, I am sharing with you some of the most valuable (and simple) insights the world has ever gleaned from the ranks of management (and rank management). The three R's are *retrain, relocate, release.*

Perhaps this person will respond to a new job that requires new skills. This could change her attitude and willingness and increase her ability. Retraining the person could offer her "a new lease on life" of a sort.

Perhaps she has had poor managers, and this has stifled her ability to use her abilities. Over time this created an unwilling attitude. In this case, you could relocate her and hope that you haven't simply shifted the problem to another department. I have discovered over the many years of my own management experience a new twist on the *caveat emptor*. (For you non-Latin scholars, *caveat emptor* means *let the buyer beware*.) The manager's version is *let the manager beware* when another manager offers to transfer one of his "key people" to the other's department when they are looking for help. Moving the problem doesn't solve the problem.

The final recourse is simply that: the final recourse. I am not a big believer in dismissing people. It shows failure all around. It ought to be the absolute, dead-bang last resort. People are too valuable to handle in this way. It can send shock waves through the department or company. It surfaces weaknesses on all sides from the hiring process to the team or manager. It can be devastating to the self-esteem of the person who is dismissed. BUT there are times when it is the best and only alternative. "Two wrongs never make a right," as they say. And keeping someone who doesn't or can't perform their responsibilities only makes the situation worse . . . for both parties.

HIGH WILLING/HIGH ABILITY

Finally we get to the win-win people. They are both willing and able to stretch and be stretched in order to maximize the success of others and themselves. They have the resiliency required to function in various roles and work out of their *comfort zones* when required to do so for certain periods of time.

They possess the kind of positive attitudes it takes to work all styles and types of people and value the opportunity to do so. They also possess the skills necessary to accomplish the task and build or maintain relationships along the way. When they don't have them or simply need to improve upon the ones they possess, they go out and get the tools or training necessary to equip themselves. They typically require little management/supervision, as they tend to be self-starters.

PERSONAL STYLE MODIFICATION

Strength of style, weakness of style, diversity of style, etc. In Chapter 5, we discussed at length, the importance of understanding personal styles. Understanding them is critical to successfully understanding yourself in terms of needs and behaviors. This is equally important in building and maintaining successful interpersonal relationships, both personal and professional. The overview chart of the four styles appears again in Figure 1.

The purpose of the previous discussion on rigidity/resiliency and willingness/ability was to set up the following one regarding personal style elasticity. Personal style elasticity is application-oriented. We take all that we learned about personal styles and personal style elasticity and use it to modify our own styles to *meet* or *accommodate the needs of others.* It is an outwardly focused action step that is proactive on our parts.

If one of our goals is to meet the needs of others to build and maintain successful relationships (and hopefully it is), then we must "bend and stretch" on occasion to do so. Let's look at some examples of personal style and style elasticity. Three key areas of the relationships between the four primary styles will be discussed. They are *conflict point(s)*, *the flex point(s)*, and some *how-to's*. I want to focus our attention on those key areas that are most likely to contribute to the success or failure of people and relationships. In addition, the composite personal styles chart is shown again as a reference (so you don't have to flip back to Chapter 5).

The High D and Relationships

You will recall that the "D" words are direct, determined, decisive, and doer. High D's don't do relationships well. They are *very independent* by nature. While this self-sufficiency certainly has its strong points, in relationships it is their biggest challenge. Why? I will ask you the same question that I always ask my audiences. What message does the independent, highly self-sufficient person send to others? The answer is four of the most crippling words in the English language . . . *I don't need you.*

UNDERSTANDING PERSONAL STYLES—NEEDS & BEHAVIORS

"D" Words
1. Direct
2. Determined
3. Decisive
4. Doer

Key Strengths
1. Results-Oriented
2. Confident

Key Weakness
1. Impatient
2. High Control

Fears: Loss of Control

Stress Release
Physical Activity

"I" Words
1. Influence
2. Inspiring
3. Impulsive
4. Interactive

Key Strengths
1. Persuasive
2. Optimistic

Key Weakness
1. Disorganized
2. Talks too much

Fears: Loss of Status

Stress Release
"Dumps their bucket"—
Express emotions/feelings

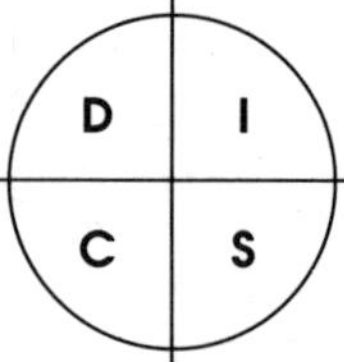

D | I

C | S

"C" Words
1. Conscientious
2. Cautious
3. Careful
4. Critical

Key Strengths
1. Analytical
2. High Standards

Key Weakness
1. Perfectionist Tendencies
2. Slow to act/decide

Fears: Being wrong;
criticism of their work

Stress Release
Time alone to reason
things out

"S" Words
1. Supportive
2. Steady
3. Sympathetic
4. Status quo

Key Strengths
1. Loyal
2. Team Player

Key Weakness
1. Resistant to change
2. Slow to act/decide

Fears: Change

Stress Release
Times alone to sleep it off

Figure 1

One of the most interesting things about this is that often High D's are unaware that they send this message. They simply like doing things themselves. Why? Because they believe they can do more, faster, by themselves. And you know what? They can. But this isn't the issue in building people and relationships. The incredible strengths the High D brings to the table (results-oriented, consummate doer, self-confidence and self-sufficiency) turn on him somewhat when applied to the relational side of life. (Remember my friend Charles Boyd's comment—weaknesses are strengths overextended.)

The conflict points for High D's are *time* and *control*. High D's simply *don't have time* for other people and relationships UNLESS they are useful in getting something done. It takes time to show someone else how to do something. They can do it faster themselves, and so they do. The down side for the High D who remains so rigid and independent is a life that is often filled with shallow or broken relationships and people. High D's tend to burn out people; others first and ultimately themselves. They're also very demanding. People tend to follow or acquiesce more out of intimidation than respect.

There are parents too busy *doing* to spend time with their families, and even when they are physically present, they aren't really there. They're on the phone with someone at the office or answering voice mail. Or they're so busy with their careers and outside activities they don't have any time left just to hang out with the kids or get involved with their school activities.

Parents (particularly us High D's), one of the tragic lessons in life that we all learn at some point is that we have a *window of opportunity* with our kids. When they are younger, they want our time and for us to be around them as much as possible. If we are too busy too long, the window closes leaving us to stand on the outside looking in, and at that point, wanting to be involved in their lives, but realizing it may be too late. They have now learned our self-sufficiency or that it isn't cool to have their parents around. So we regret that which we cannot change . . . the past. The answer lies in changing what we can . . . the present.

The second conflict point for the High D is control. This weakness was discussed previously in the chapter on personal styles. It really becomes a huge potential conflict point in interpersonal relationships. The goal of the High D is to exercise control in matters that are important to her. This controlling nature causes all kinds of problems in relationships from wars with other High D's over who's in control, to co-dependencies with the I's and S's (the people pleasers).

The obvious flex points are *making time* and *giving up control*. The real issue, though, is seeing the need to do so. Many High D's will read this material (skim it quickly) and think it applies to the other High D's they know; not to themselves. We learn to make time for the things that we value and consider important. So return to the exercise in the *values* chapter and analyze where you are spending your time. We also need to understand that those with whom we work and live know all too well the answers *and* where they fit in our scheme of priorities.

Regarding giving up control, I offer the following advice. A real paradigm shift is required here. You must first see the damage that occurs from High Control people. Secondly, you must begin to *value and appreciate the diversity of style* your teammates at work and family members bring to the table.

A final word on our High D friends. They love to compete. They compete for control or to win at just about everything they take on. The problem is that competition produces *win/lose outcomes*. We don't need more losers in relationships. This book is about building people who win by helping others win. When High D's understand and make this paradigm shift, the *results* can be truly awesome.

The High I and Relationships

You will recall the "I" words were influence, inspire, impulsive, interactive. High I's are the consummate party people. Wherever they go, they take their own party with them. We like to joke that the way to really antagonized a High I is to have a party and *not* invite them! They'll go crazy trying to get themselves included and, if all else fails, they may show up anyway.

High I's just *want to be liked*. This is their strongest felt need. Much of their self-esteem is tied to their perception of how well they are liked and the recognition they receive. Personal status is important. So how do they function relationally? Very well, in most instances. They love people and being around people. In fact, they typically hate being alone. The High I business traveler who is staying in a hotel alone will often invite themselves to dinner with a total stranger if he thinks he may have to do the unthinkable . . . eat alone. They've been known to invite the servers in the restaurant to join them.

Because of their optimistic, outgoing and expressive style, High I's typically draw other people to themselves. They quickly blend in with groups and often provide the energy and entertainment. They love to laugh and have fun. This can be contagious to other people, and most of us like that. They tend to have a natural persuasive quality, and thus are good at rallying people around a cause or purpose such as in a team dynamic at work. High I's like interacting with groups of people. And the more the merrier. They tend to focus more on breadth of relationships rather than depth. This means they *know* a lot of people a little bit. They have many *best friends*.

So what possible relationship down-side could exist with these wonderful people? Like all of us, High I's are not without their interpersonal challenges. While not as challenging as those of the High D we just discussed, nevertheless, they do exist. The conflict points involve *the need for approval* and *recognition*. The two are obviously linked.

Most people want to be liked. Most people seek the approval of others. But High I's really *need them*. We see a particular characteristic early in High I children that sometimes carries over into their adult lives. It is competing for the *attention* and *recognition* of their parents. When the High I child sees a sibling or another child get a laugh or do something that draws attention, she immediately does the exact same thing. Our oldest son used to do this a lot. We had to continually remind him that whatever it was his sister or brother did was only cute or funny once or when it was spontaneous. He was reminding us of his need for our attention.

As with the High D, this competition can lead to unhealthy win/ lose outcomes. The High I tends to take things more personally. They feel personally rejected when they don't win. Winning is defined as getting the recognition, attention, or approval they believe is due them. Taken to extremes, they may become *approval addicts.* (I first came across this expression reading Robert McGee's book, *The Search for Significance.*)

This over-zealous desire for recognition and approval can lead to problems in relationships. For example, at the office this person may always be perceived as positioning himself for the "big win." He may take credit when it is due someone else. He tends to get labeled as *political* and *self-serving.*

The flex points involve dealing with these approval and recognition issues. First, let's look at how to deal with the approval one. I dealt with the *personal* side of this issue in Chapter 5. We deal with the *inter-personal* side here in much the same way. It begins with self-approval. This is not self-worship. It is actually very solid theology as well as psychology. The High I must learn to get comfortable with who he is from the strengths of his style to its inherent weaknesses.

It is difficult to build successful relationships that endure difficult times if you disapprove of yourself. We have to learn that our attitudes cannot be solidly linked to the approval/disapproval of others. No doubt it is to some extent for all of us, particularly High I's. BUT we must get to the point where we can handle rejection without so internalizing it that we wreck our self-esteem and attitude. The inability to do so can lead to some pretty serious conditions (e.g. depression, co-dependencies and other dysfunctional problems).

When I first started my company, I loved to do everything except sell. Why? I suffered from the two most classic conditions that many rookie and some veteran sales people do: call reluctance and fear of rejection. Call reluctance is partially related to the approval problem, while fear of rejection is strongly related. You could call it *fear of being disapproved.* The key to solving this is to learn not to take it personally; to be able to differentiate between the person and the product or service.

So remember, that while we all like to be approved by others—particularly those with whom we are most closely linked, the fact is "it ain't always gonna be so." We must separate criticism of *what we do* from *who we are*. And finally, we must understand that there are always going to be people who can't be pleased no matter what we do. Different values, different spiritual centers, and different personal styles all cause different agendas and motivations.

The recognition issue is absolutely related to the discussion above. But in addition, High I's need to learn the value of passing along the recognition to others; even if it means they get less. High I's are confrontation avoiders, particularly if they think it could embarrass them or cause a loss of status. Too often they want to "duck the pie in the face" and let the person behind them take it.

Learning to "duck" some of the recognition to let others catch it is a real trust and relationship builder. Someone has said "it is amazing what people can accomplish if it doesn't matter who gets the credit." When High I's buy into this, amazing and positive things happen.

The High S and Relationships

You will recall the "S" words were supportive, steady, sympathetic, and status quo. There are a number of similarities between the High S and the High I as both are people-oriented. You recall from our discussion in Chapter 5 that the difference was primarily one of how you answered the "HOW" questions. Fast/slow, hurried/deliberate. It is an issue of speed. The High S is slower and more deliberate in her approach to life.

Another difference is the level of relationships. Remember we said that High I's had breadth of relationships (knowing a lot of people a little). The High S seeks *depth of relationship*. They typically have fewer, but closer, friends. The High S prefers the small group to the large one; the more intimate dinner with close friends rather than the large banquet. One of the real strengths of this style that is invaluable in relationships is their High Degree of loyalty. One of Solomon's proverbs says "There is a friend who sticks closer than a brother." This could be said of our High S friends. When you need them, they always seem to be around.

In terms of needs in a relationship, the High S *needs to feel accepted and appreciated.* I know this sounds a lot like the High I who we said needs approval and recognition, but there are some differences. Understanding these differences is one of the real keys to building successful, lasting relationships with these people.

It took some doing, but I finally came up with a couple of dictionary definitions that (for the purposes of this discussion) help differentiate *approval* and *acceptance.* Approval means *favorable regard; commendation.* It is more outward or overt. The commendation part of the definition ties very well into the recognition need of the High I. It is the visible type of up front recognition.

On the other hand, acceptance is defined as *belief in something; agreement.* It has a more internal feel to it. Since the High S is very trusting and works hard to build trust-based relationships, the words *belief in* are a key part. One of the key distinctions that needs to be made is the difference between recognition and appreciation, the latter being the key to successful relationships with the High S.

Since Gigi (my wife) has a High S component to her style, she has, over the years, served as a good source of information regarding this. In addition, when doing programs that involve personal style profiles, I always ask the High S people in my audiences to help the others understand what appreciation means. The response is consistent. Appreciation has more to do with showing people you care, not in the demonstrative ways that excite the High I, but in the little, subtle ways that communicate respect, value, gratitude and love.

Again, some of you are probably thinking, surely *these* people have no inter-personal or relationship problems. And as it was with the High I, my response is "not exactly true." Potential conflict points do exist. They arise from three areas: *indecisiveness, resistance to change,* and *the need for acceptance taken to extremes.*

Indecisiveness may not seem like a big deal to most of us, but it can be a source of irritation and cause problems in relationships. I always think of the young couple sitting in the car on their first date and the conversation goes something like . . . "Where would you like to go for dinner?" "Oh, I don't care, where would you like to go?" "It really doesn't matter to me, why don't you choose?" "No really it doesn't matter to me, I'm easy to please . . ." And so on, until it gets to be about 10:00 p.m., and they finally decide to just order in pizza. The trouble is for some people this carries into our business and family relationships, and it can create problems.

Resistance to change is another one of those areas that on the surface seems innocent enough. But in today's rapidly changing corporate world (and even our personal lives), change is the only remaining constant. Relationships, like the people in them, can become so rigid that when they get even a little stressed (stretched) they break or get permanently bent out of shape. Those who insist on doing everything the way "good old mom or dad" did, whether it is running your business or your home, may be setting themselves up for some difficult times.

The third conflict point is an interesting one that parallels to a large extent the approval addicts discussion regarding the High I. The reason is because both of these styles are people-oriented. The problem manifests itself differently with the High S. The High S tends to see confrontation and disagreement as having only negative outcomes. They are perceived to divide rather than unite people. This certainly may be the case, but it doesn't have to be. When a person has this mindset, they often retreat or simply keep silent about things that may be important to them. This creates obvious problems. But they usually don't surface until later. Sometimes to the other person/people involved, the issue was past and forgotten. Then, seemingly out of nowhere, it resurfaces. It is brought up out of sheer frustration by the hurt High S who could hold it in no longer.

The flex points here may seem to some, pretty straightforward, but they really do represent a challenge to the High S. First, learning to make decisions even if the outcome could cause problems in the future. Our High S friends have probably experienced enough of the negative results of indecisiveness. It is time they were able to enjoy the fruit of a well-considered decision. Their motives and agendas tend to be purer and fairer than any of the other styles because of their inherent nature to help and support others. The High S needs to recognize this about themselves. Other observant people certainly do. So even if something does go wrong or the outcome of a decision turns sour, remember the three F's from Chapter 7, *forgive, forget* and *forge ahead*, and then get on with your life.

Regarding resistance to change, the High S must come to grips with the reality of change. If not, their relationships will suffer. This fact, in itself, can be a motivating factor for the High S. They need to do something wild and crazy like buying a new toothbrush even though all the bristles haven't fallen out yet. Re-grip your golf clubs and re-spike your shoes, you wild and crazy guy. Sit in a different pew in the church, if you dare.

For those of you involved with our High S friends, remember this important truth about *change* and the High S. They can and will change IF we help them understand the reasons why and the expected outcomes. AND most importantly, we must give them time to assimilate the change. Don't walk in tomorrow and inform your mate that you think the family ought to move across country. Or don't be cruel at work by announcing that "there are going to be some changes around here, and we won't know for a few months though if you'll keep your jobs." This type of timing may cause *panic attacks* and *bridge jumping* in those whose S is extremely high.

Finally, we come to the point of dealing with confrontation and disagreement. The High S must come to the realization that conflict and disagreement can be healthy in the right environment and under the right circumstances. Since the High S builds trust-based relationships, they really should feel more secure in dealing with these inevitable issues. The High S is also very well equipped to use one of her strengths in the most important aspect of conflict resolution: *time*. The High S has more patience than any other style and has the *ability* to work through things if she will also demonstrate the *willingness*.

The High C and Relationships

You will recall the "C" words were conscientious, cautious, careful, and critical. We have returned to a personal style that is *task focused* rather than *people-oriented*. So the High C parallels more the High D than the other two as it relates to focus. On the "HOW" they do things side, they are slower and more deliberate like their High S counterparts. You may also recall that their self-esteem is heavily tied to maintaining very high quality standards and their attention to detail. They are highly analytical by nature and tend to question everything; asking the "WHY" questions. They hate to be wrong, so they usually believe *the right way is their way.*

From a relationship point of view, their potential conflict points come out of these areas: very high quality standards, over-analyzing and questioning everything, the need to always be right, and doing things their way. Let's look at each in a little more detail.

It is a fine thing to have and maintain High Standards of excellence both personally and professionally. It is a true sign of outstanding character. So, how does this lead to inter-personal problems? To answer that, we need to briefly re-visit our discussion of expectations. You may recall I discussed at length the person whose standards (expectations) were so high that even they couldn't meet them. We later discussed how this can naturally lead to relationship problems. How? If I can't live up to or meet my own expectations, then how can anyone else? The answer is—*they can't.* We set up ourselves and others to fail in this scenario, and thus we have little or no chance for success in relationships.

There are many people in life who take most everything "at face value." They typically accept what people tell them without raising issues or getting into lengthy discussions. Not so with the High C. They are the *questions* people of the world. To them, everything is open for discussion unless perhaps they have already done exhaustive research on the subject and *convinced themselves* one way or the other. This causes problems in relationships.

To compound matters, their analytical nature gets them into difficulties in the area of decision making much like the High S. They are slow to act or decide. The phrase "paralysis of analysis" was coined about High C's (certainly not by one though). They will usually argue that they need more time to gather data or study the situation using "quality of results" as the reason (or excuse).

The *need to be right* is a real *relationship choker*. This is directly related to the High C's need for *security* and *respect* from relationships. High C's are very cautious in relationships. They tend to be "close to the vest" with their feelings and have a difficult time expressing them. This need to be right also makes them more argumentative than others. Put two High C's in a room together to discuss a subject in which they are both knowledgeable, and they could spend the rest of eternity discussing/arguing it, trying to prove who is the *rightest!*

Doing things *their way* is very much related to *being the rightest* for this simple reason. If the High C was right or had the best argument, then why wouldn't it follow that we would choose his way to carry out the next steps and implement his solution? Seems obvious enough, right? Unfortunately for the High C, some people don't reason or draw their conclusions and inferences the same way. Thus they arrive at *different* ones.

The *flex points* again become obvious, based on the High C characteristics discussed above. First, reread the pages in the chapter on expectations that deal with this issue of *too high* expectations. Then go through the exercise on examining your expectations in terms of the three keys: *realistic, control,* and *ownership.*

Next, we need to become *unparalyzed.* It is not only okay to make a decision, it is a must. Too many opportunities are missed personally and professionally by people waiting to get just another piece of information that would let them make a "higher quality decision." Business opportunities are missed and business failures occur every day because someone wanted to "run the numbers one more time or examine them from another set of parameters."

Whether the audience is corporate, association, or a marriage conference, I am often asked by husbands and wives how to deal with this issue in marriage. They see or are feeling the negative impacts of *indecision* on their marriage or with their children. One of the best pieces of advice you can give the High C is *decide to decide.*

If someone is always right, then everyone else is always wrong (unless they happen to agree with you). What have you automatically created? Another win/lose scenario. Relationships survive and thrive on things like open, two-way communication, understanding, sometimes consensus and sometimes compromise, expressing feelings to each other, among other things. Too often in the world of the analytical High C, things are black and white. They would do well to learn to see the shades of gray that exist all around them. Their ability to flex here is critical to *maintaining* long term, healthy relationships.

"My way or the highway." This was a popular corporate phrase used in the 70s and early 80s of managers who always had to be right, whose way had to be best, and if you didn't agree you could work elsewhere. There are some real relationship potholes on this road. First, if one of our goals as a leader is to help people think for themselves and really feel and act empowered, then this approach is totally wrong.

Think about this as it relates to raising our kids. We want them to learn to be responsible citizens as they grow and mature. But how can they if we make all their decisions for them or force them to do everything the way we would do them or want them done? The answer is—*they can't.* Super High Control parents can cause all kinds of problems for their kids from co-dependencies to outright rebellion. Don't misunderstand. I am all for parental involvement, ground rules and guidelines, but *flexibility is a real key to success.* This is particularly true as they get older.

Similar things happen when we manage the people with whom we work in this way. I do a lot of *empowerment* programs. From this experience dealing with the people that are supposed to be *becoming empowered,* I find that many are skeptical. Why? It's pretty simple. They know or believe that when the program is over they will return to the office and the same old High Control, *do it the way I told you to* manager (who didn't have to attend the program) will be there to greet them. This continues to amaze me, and I see it or hear about it frequently. The chapter on empowerment will address this type of issue in more detail.

Finally, this *my way* business really *stifles creativity*. We hear a lot about creativity and risk taking today in the corporate world; more so from those who write about what it ought to be like than those who have to practice it. Creative people need flexible managers who allow them to pursue different paradigms for new solutions. When High C's make this shift (personally and professionally), combined with their natural process thinking abilities, real breakthroughs can occur and solid relationships can be built.

SOME FINAL WORDS ON PERSONAL STYLE ELASTICITY

To close this lengthy and important chapter, I thought I would offer a few useful tips and observations gathered over the years to help you apply these principles in your relationships.

First, people *choose* to modify their styles or demonstrate style elasticity. It is a voluntary decision. Some will choose to do nothing; remaining rigid and inflexible. In essence, they are choosing to fail or maintain mediocre relationships. I encourage you to choose success by choosing to stretch and be stretched.

Second, it is a *temporary* modification. You can't live for extended periods of time "outside your comfort zone." Stretching and flexing can be stressful. Resiliency (that quality or ability to return to the original shape after being stretched) is one of the keys to your personal success.

Third, we need to recognize and remind ourselves that different people have varying degrees of *willingness* and *ability*. You can control your own attitude. You can only influence the attitudes of others. You can't change them. Only they can do that.

Fourth, we must remain *teachable*. I have alluded to this several times in the various discussions. Being teachable means we are willing to be *continuous learners*. To stop learning is to stop growing. It also is an attitude indicator.

Finally, maturity and balance are real *facilitators* of success in style elasticity. Maturity means *highly developed*. Most of us realize now that as we get older and gain more experience, we learn some of these lessons even when we weren't necessarily trying to. Over time, our perspectives tend to broaden. Some of the sharp edges of our personal styles that used to cause pain in relationships have been rounded off. This is maturity. Balance in our spiritual, emotional, and physical lives gives us the freedom to stretch (and be stretched) and the resiliency to return comfortably home again.

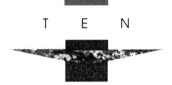

Understanding and Influence . . . Power Tools for Motivating Others

"Motivation is the art of getting someone to do something you want them to do because they want to do it."

D. D. EISENHOWER

"I like Ike," read the campaign slogan for the 1956 presidential campaign. Since I was but a small boy at that time, I can only say I like his quotation about motivating others. It sums up the message of this chapter in one sentence. You will recall in Chapter 6, we discussed *personal* empowerment and motivation. I introduced the concept of the *personal operating system* and tied it to *talents, roles,* and *goals.* The focus was you . . . *what turns your crank.*

This chapter is dedicated to those who really want to understand what it takes to apply this information and make it work, not just personally, but *inter-personally.* People everywhere ask the question, "How do I motivate others?" "How do I motivate those who work for me, those with whom I work, my mate, my children?" The answer is simpler than most people expect. The answer is—*you don't.* Said another way—*you can't.*

You're probably thinking to yourself, if that is his answer, this is going to be the shortest (and least helpful) chapter in the book. That isn't my intention or design. While I firmly believe you can't and don't motivate others, there are two things you can do. Using these two tools with people you want to motivate can have a very profound impact on them and the results they produce. The two tools are *understanding* and *influence*.

UNDERSTANDING

To perceive and comprehend the nature and significance of; grasp. Figure 1 shows the Personal Operating System diagram we discussed previously in Chapter 6. In discussing it, I said that understanding the individual components and their relationships was critical to personal empowerment. Well, when it comes to motivating others, *understanding* is one of the tools for success. This time the understanding is not of your own personal operating system, but that of others. You want to know what turns their crank? Start by trying to understand their personal operating system.

Before developing this point further, we need to understand that "understanding" *does not* mean agreement with or ownership of someone else's personal operating system. It *does mean* that we grasp the nature and significance of it *to them* (not to us). People are motivated by what's important to themselves. They do things for their reasons, not ours.

Understanding personal style issues, values, character, and spiritual center give us insight and perspective we need to help motivate them. Some of you may be thinking, this is a very personal thing, like religion or something. You are right. Hopefully you gained some insight and perspective regarding the personal side of this in Chapter 6. Motivation is, indeed, a personal thing.

In order to help motivate someone, we must have some form of a relationship with that person. This doesn't mean we have to be "bosom buddies" or even close friends, but some type of working relationship must be there. Understanding another person's personal operating system helps begin to build a bridge to that person. It communicates respect. Remember we said *respect demonstrates that we value the person, even if we don't value their values.*

Understanding (or at least attempting to) adds support to the bridge. Many of us can relate to the *generation gap*, particularly if you're a "boomer." For my generation, it was the one we dealt with

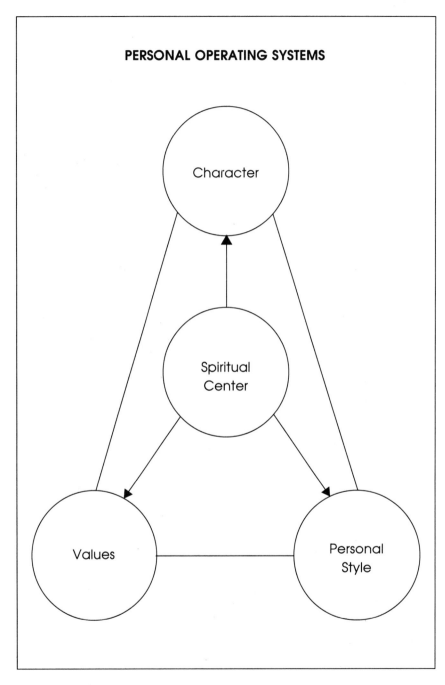

Figure 1

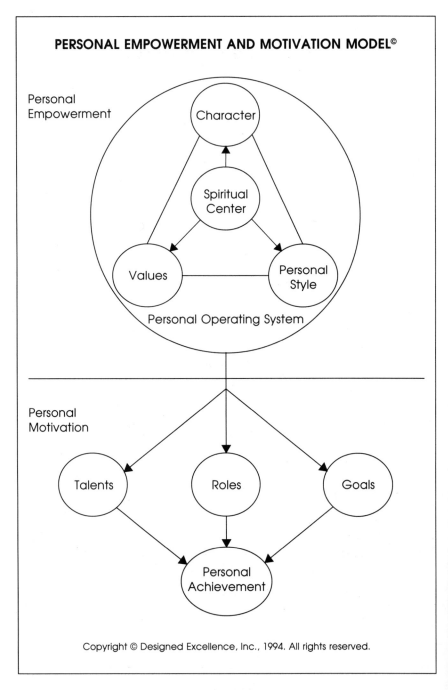

PERSONAL EMPOWERMENT AND MOTIVATION MODEL©

Personal Empowerment

Character

Spiritual Center

Values

Personal Style

Personal Operating System

Personal Motivation

Talents

Roles

Goals

Personal Achievement

Figure 2

in the late 60s and early 70s. You may now be on the other side of the "gap" if you are dealing with your own teenagers or *generation Xer's* (as they are called by the media). (Sorry friends, since I got a later start in life raising my kids than most of you did, I have yet to reach that point. I pray you survive, if only to write your own book and tell me *how to* when the time comes!)

What some of us remember about this time in our own lives was this *understanding* business. Or should I say the lack of it. For those of us who can remember *way back then*, who doesn't remember the parents and teachers we thought were cool, and those who weren't? While we didn't realize it at the time, we were defining *cool*. We defined it as those who took the time, and at least tried, to understand our point of view or position, no matter how ridiculous it seemed to them at the time (and to many of us now). We simply wanted to be understood. And for those of us who never felt like we were, we brought (and bring) more baggage to our relationships.

So if we've applied the *three F* tools (*forgiving, forgetting,* and *forging ahead*), and we are reasonably mature in our *style elasticity*, we are in a tremendous, somewhat unique, position. We are positioned to *understand* others and use this understanding to help build successful relationships and people. The way we do this is through one of the most powerful tools, and yet one of the softest; *influence*.

INFLUENCE

A power affecting a person, thing, or course of events. Herein lies the power to help motivate others. I maintained earlier that we really can't *influence* to change the personal operating systems of most *mature* adults. Rather, we should concentrate on the *understanding side* in that arena.

Now we move into a discussion of the arena that we can, and must, influence *if* we want to "motivate" others. In Chapter 6, I called that arena *personal motivation*. It includes the motivation factors: talents, roles, and goals that lead to personal achievement. (See Figure 2.)

We are only going to consider *positive influence* in this chapter. I said previously that influence is soft, but don't misunderstand. Consider how the Colorado river has *influenced* the Grand Canyon over the many thousands of years. Consider also the profound influence Abraham Lincoln, a gentle, soft-spoken man, had on our nation with regard to abolition of one of our nation's greatest shames. We can and do influence people. We can "motivate" them by influencing their personal motivating factors. Let's consider how.

Talents

When given the opportunity, people love to talk about their talents (provided they understand them). They do this, not in an arrogant way, but in a positive one. For those who are still unable to do so, this may represent a self-esteem issue. But for those who do understand them, and can be made comfortable discussing them, we have an I.O. (and I don't mean input/output). I mean an *influence opportunity.*

One of the most motivating things in life is not *knowing* your talents, but *using them. People are motivated by opportunities to use their talents.* Win/win situations are created when we are not only allowed to use them, but encouraged to do so.

The flip side is people stagnating in their personal and professional lives. And we all know that over time, stagnant water "stinks up the place." So it is with stagnant people. So why not give people the opportunity to come out "smelling like a rose?"

Stewardship. This is a word that means a lot to me personally and professionally. I define it as *taking care of and judicious use of that which has been entrusted to you.* I believe this should be applied to talents. This applies to those who possess the talents and those of us who lead/manage those with the talents.

Good stewards use their talents wisely. The end result usually includes having helped or served someone else's needs along the way. Good managers help people develop their talents. The truly empowered manager has a knack for recognizing them in others, *and* providing an environment in which they can grow. Why? Because she knows that this is one of her ways to maximize another I.O. (influence opportunity).

Roles

We know from our previous discussion of roles in Chapter 6, different people prefer different roles in life. Some are supporters who prefer the "behind the scenes" activities. Others like it up front on the leading edge and enjoy the accompanying risk. Others still feel safest in the middle ground.

Having just made a case for the fact that people are motivated when they get to use their talents, let me now build on this by adding another component. *People are highly motivated by opportunities to use their talents in the roles they prefer*. This is true personally and professionally.

My work with organizations in the areas of *empowerment initiatives* and *strategic development of high performance teams* has lead to some interesting studies and even more interesting findings. I consider none of them revolutionary and perhaps only reinforcing what many would say they knew already, but nonetheless useful for this discussion.

Particularly within team dynamics, there is considerable talk about and activity concerning *team member* and *team leadership* roles. We often find teams swapping or alternating roles in terms of ongoing responsibilities including team leadership. This is typically associated with a fair amount of cross-training.

One of the potentially challenging issues for these people occurs when members are asked to function in roles that are not "to their liking." The mature, highly style-elastic team member will often "suck it up" for the sake of the team, at least for a while. But over time, the stress level goes up and the motivation level goes down. Why? Usually it is because the role isn't congruent with personal style, talents, or perhaps their personal goals. In some cases, it is a combination of these.

Organizations demonstrate good stewardship and wisdom when they understand the role(s) that best suit their people. People in senior management positions particularly need to pay attention to this. I am not minimizing the role of others in the various levels of the organization. Rather I want to emphasize the absolute importance of *role management* at those levels from which comes much of the overall vision and direction for the organization.

Goals

Permit me to add one more *piece of tail to the kite*. This piece is about goals and goal setting. Our statement about motivation now reads: *People are most highly motivated by opportunities to use their talents in the roles they prefer when working toward goals they own.* You will find you have to hold them back. They pursue them with *passion*. When is the last time you pursued something passionately. If the last time you did so was during your courtship and you've been married for over ten years, may I suggest you need a refresher course!

People feel passionately about things they own. Not everything they own, but those that are congruent with their personal operating systems, utilize their talents, *and* provide a role they enjoy. This creates passion. You know what else? It doesn't even have to be a goal they thought up themselves, like catching a record-breaking bass or shooting a round in the 70s. It can be one of the company's goals! Do you believe this? It's true!

As long as your goals (or those of the organization) are congruent with your people's personal goals (meet the criteria above), the transfer of ownership can be made. How? Here are a couple of ways to get you started. First, understand their personal goals. If you don't do this, you've failed this chapter miserably and have to go back and re-read the *Understanding* section.

Second, look for the areas of congruence between their goals and yours (the organizations) and help them see these areas. Make it clear how their talents can be utilized and how valuable they are to your success. If possible, place them in roles that work to their strengths and maximize their chances for success.

Third (and most importantly), answer the *WIIFM* question. *What's in it for me?* Or in this case, what's in it for them? Everyone wants to know the rewards for winning and/or the consequences of not achieving the desired outcome. It is essential that these rewards (or the contrary) be meted out fairly and consistently. It also helps if the same rules apply to everyone. Again, I call this to the attention of the senior executives. This is where most initiatives from *empowerment to employee involvement to performance management* fall very short of the target; at least according to the feedback I get from your people "in the ranks."

Remember: *People are* most highly *motivated by opportunities to use their talents in the roles they prefer when working toward goals they own.* And the exciting thing is that those who lead/manage your organization can cause this to happen by creating and managing I.O.'s.

PART THREE

Finishing Tools for Smoothing Out the Rough Spots

INTRODUCTION

Ever wonder why, when you're running down the stairs in your house and slide your hand down the banister rail to keep your balance, you didn't get a hand full of splinters? The answer is simple, the carpenter *finished* the job.

He didn't stop with just making it out of a 4"x4" piece of wood and then mount it along side the stairs on top of the spindles. He understood *how* it was to be used by those who were building the house. He anticipated the man and woman of the house hurrying down the stairs (clinging tightly to the banister) to get someplace they were supposed to be thirty minutes ago. He remembered his own small children running down the stairs Christmas morning to see what toys had been left for them under the tree (clinging tightly to the banister to keep their balance).

He remembered he and his wife fussing at the kids for sliding down their old banister. They warned the kids many times that they could get a bottom full of splinters, but he knew they really wouldn't because the carpenter had finished his work.

He stood reflecting fondly on his daughter's first prom. He remembered how she came down the stairs clinging so tightly to the banister, awkwardly negotiating them in her new heels. He remembered, too, her young escort as he clung to the rail at the bottom of the stairs. He wondered who would faint first as their nervous states became even more apparent.

But through all these things, no splinters . . . because the carpenter had finished his work. When two pieces of wood are joined together, it is nearly impossible to get an exact fit. No matter how skilled the carpenter or how sharp or powerful the tool, there are almost always some rough edges that have to be dealt with. To deal with them most effectively takes a gentle touch of one with experience and caring. Carpenters use things like emery cloth or very fine grit sandpaper to blend the two together, smoothing out the rough spots.

So it is with people and relationships. When two people are put together, whether in a high performance team in a corporate setting, or in a marriage, there are always going to be rough spots. There will always be those "ends" that don't quite fit together. Today, too many of us would "force fit" the pieces together or quit trying altogether. When things don't fit together the way we think they should, sometimes we find the biggest sledge hammer we can and begin to *beat the health* out of them until they finally "fit."

These last chapters provide some emery cloth to help you smooth out the rough spots and soften the sharp edges. They were written to help us continue to work on smoothing out our relationships. These tools will help gently massage your relationships to improve their condition. They should also help keep them smooth as you weather the storms that will surely come your way. I hope through their use you will give and get fewer splinters in your hands and especially your bottoms!

Pulling Splinters . . .
Dig Out Your Own Before
You Go Picking at Mine!

"Why do you look at the splinter that is in your brother's eye,
and not notice the log that is in your own?"

JESUS CHRIST

P ulling splinters is tough work. It can be a painful process. Be
cause it is, I'd rather do it *for* you than have you do it *to* me.
Splinters are interesting little pests. They are usually pretty
small in size. Some hurt more than others. It seems to depend somewhat on how deep under the skin they get. And if left unattended,
they can fester and become infected, leading to some real pain.

Everyone has probably "dug out" a splinter or two from his or her
own body or from someone else's at some point in our lives. This
past summer, Gracie (my daughter) had been running outside barefoot. I never have been much for going barefoot because I am a real
tenderfoot, and I stub my toes a lot. (That hurts worse than splinters.) Since Gracie has a bit of "Ellie Mae Clampett" in her, she likes
going barefoot. Well, anyway, she came hopping into the house on
one foot crying and screaming as she had gotten a pretty sizable
splinter in her foot.

As usual, she was looking for her mom to comfort her and pain-
lessly remove the intruder. Unfortunately for her, mom wasn't at
home, but I was. She deliberated waiting in pain for mom to get
home versus enduring the pain her dad with the "touch of Conan"
might inflict upon her. I chose the latter for her.

I really did try to make it as painless as possible. I got out the "splinter digging" needle and alcohol. After sterilizing the needle, I reached for her foot as she screamed louder. As I raised the needle to her foot, she really let go with an ear-piercer. I told her I hadn't even touched it yet, so she calmed down a little. I finally managed to remove the splinter, and fortunately for both of us it didn't hurt much. As a matter of fact when I told her I was done, she yelled back to me "That wasn't so bad, Dad," as she ran out to play again. I guess sometimes short memories are a blessing.

Isn't it amazing how much easier it is to dig a splinter out of *someone else's* foot or hand? When we use "splinters" *metaphorically* with other people's "faults" as it is used in the quote above, we get a picture of why that seems to be the case. If I see my faults or shortcomings at all, I tend to see them as specks of dust or small splinters. When I examine yours, they appear to me as large as logs. They seem so evident to me, I wonder why you can't see them? In His discussion, Christ offers the different perspective discussed in Chapter 2. The splinter is in the other person's eye, the log in our own.

SPLITTING MY LOGS

Here I would like to challenge us to examine our own lives first; give ourselves an annual check-up of sorts. If I deal with my *logs*, some interesting things happen to the other person's splinters.

In the great Northwest, lumberjacking has long been a source of income and competition. One day a strong, young lumberjack challenged the older, reigning champion to a log splitting contest. Whoever could split the most logs in one eight hour shift would be the winner.

The young lumberjack worked feverishly throughout the day, stopping only to get an occasional, quick drink of water and snarf down a sandwich for lunch. The older man stopped more frequently and for longer periods of time to rest. At the end of the day, much to the amazement and chagrin of the young challenger, the older man's wood pile was considerably higher than his own.

Disappointed and dismayed, the young man asked the champion how we had done it; how could he split more logs stopping more often and for longer periods of time? The wise, older man replied, "Every time I took a break, I also took time out to re-sharpen my ax."

In one of the best books written in my lifetime, *Seven Habits of Highly Effective People*, Stephen Covey's seventh habit is "Sharpen the Saw." If you haven't reread it recently, I suggest you do so. It deals masterfully with what he refers to as the "four dimensions of renewal."

My purpose here is to suggest a few things we can do to deal with some of our own "logs." It begins with what the wise log splitting champion talked about as being critical to his success—re-sharpening his ax. Let's examine what he did.

MAKING TIME TO STOP

He made the time to do what was required to win. Notice I didn't say he *found* the time.

If you are like me, finding more time would be nice but there are still only twenty-four hours in a day and most people sleep about a third of that. Believe me when I say, we aren't going to find anymore time. BUT we can *make* time available for what's most important.

Notice that the first thing the older lumberjack did was *not* slow down. Many people today encourage us to slow down, ease up or chill out. That is not what he did. He *stopped*. Sometimes you just have to stop. Slowing down just won't get it! Have you ever been stopped by a police officer for running a stop sign and discussed the oxymoron . . . *making a rolling stop*. There is no such thing as you will learn when you pay the fine for *making a rolling stop*.

It is difficult to accomplish much in a quality manner "on the fly." We all need *quiet times* in our lives to reflect internally. Time in which we stop. "And do nothing?" you ask. No. This time we make for "stops" takes on different purposes for different people. For me, this is a quiet time alone with my God; a time of solitude and spiritual renewal. For others, again depending on your spiritual center, it is more a time of solitude and meditating on things. Without this time, we can't sharpen the ax because, like the young lumberjack, we don't think or know that it needs it.

How much time? Different people suggest different amounts of time. Covey suggests at least an hour a day, others suggest more, some less, others still suggest grabbing *time bytes* during the day to stop periodically at frequent intervals. The latter makes it difficult to really process things, and this is a process. I don't know what will work best for you or what time of day. You must determine that for yourself. I'm an early morning person, while others prefer the evening or night. Just make the time, use it wisely, and be consistent.

EXAMINING THE TOOLS HELPS MAINTAIN A "BALANCED" LIFE

Once he sat down, the lumberjack examined the condition of his ax. Handle O.K.? Check. Head secured on? Check. Cutting edge sharp? No. Then he gets out the whetstone or wheel and sharpens it again. How about you? How often do check to see if your personal edge remains sharp while the joints of your relationships remain tight and smooth.

In the first part of this book, I discussed a number of areas of your *personal* life that need to be understood by you and brought into congruence in order for you to optimize your chances for success. Maintaining *balance* in these areas should be one of our highest personal goals.

How do we define balance? How about something simple like "the ability to remain upright; to keep from falling down." One of the best synonyms for it that most of us can relate to is *sanity*. How do we maintain our sanity? For some, life is so hectic at times that simply maintaining our sanity (emotional/mental balance) is a major undertaking.

Let's examine personal balance in light of the five primary subject matters discussed in Part One of the book.

Character

Remember our discussion of the *being side* vs. *the doing side?* Losing our balance here usually means that we have gone too far toward the doing side. I also discussed six key characteristics of people of positively outstanding character: respect, integrity, honesty, moral absolutes, responsibility and courage.

When we get out of balance from the character point of view, it manifests itself through a very ugly creature known as *compromise.* This can be moral, ethical, or spiritual compromise. It is an expedient road to travel, but the journey back is a long and difficult one. And the trip is not often forgotten.

Expectations

Next, we discussed expectations from both personal and interpersonal points of view. I know when my personal expectations are out of balance because I get frustrated and angry with myself for not living up to my (too high) expectations. Similarly, we know we are out of balance in our expectations of others when we begin to *criticize* them for not meeting our expectations of them. This criticism has two forms: *overt* and *covert.*

Overt criticism is that which we personally deliver to another person. Covert criticism is more subtle. It usually exists primarily in the mind of the person whose high expectations went unmet. It is damaging to the person internalizing it. When we do this, we waste too much time and energy *making mountains out of molehills.* During this process, we also typically continue to diminish the esteem we once held for this person who disappointed us so.

Rather than criticize and dwell on the negative, we need to revisit the three expectation checkpoints: *reality, control,* and *ownership* to restore balance. We must again ask ourselves, was it realistic? Who controlled the outcome? Who owned the expectation? Unless we can satisfactorily answer these, they can become *logs* in our lives that must be dealt with later.

Values

The third major area of discussion was that of *personal values*. I said that our personal values determine *why* we do what we do. This one appears on the surface to be harder to discern an out of balance condition. For some it is the old "nailing gelatin to a tree" scenario again. How do you know when your values are out of balance? What does it look like? I believe the answer lies more in *what does it feel like?* The key is in our internal *feelings*.

You may recall earlier we briefly discussed a concept that I referred to as *the peace factor*. It is a peace of mind kind of thing. Do I seem to lack the peace/contentment factor? This is too "warm and fuzzy" for some to process. Another way of looking at it is in terms of *internal conflict*. Do I feel like there is a *battle of the minds* going on within my mind? If so, I suggest you re-visit the values clarification exercise. Compare your top three values with where you are right now, what you are doing, and most importantly, why you are doing what you are doing.

A personal example may be helpful to your understanding of this less *concrete* area. One of the things I value most is my quiet time, mentioned previously. It has been a regular, consistent part of my life for about seventeen years. If I get out of synch in terms of schedule, as can occur when I'm on the road, I may miss these times. However, if I miss more than a day or two, it creates a sense of internal conflict, and the peace factor leaves. Why? Because I am not living consistently in terms of that which I highly value.

Let me leave you with an important thought to remember. "Out of balance" values that go unchecked for long periods of time ultimately lead to character compromise. This is one you need to not only consider, but commit to memory. It becomes a steady erosion process if not kept in balance.

Personal Style Issues

Our fourth subject matter dealt with the area of personal style issues. We examined the strengths and weaknesses of these four needs-based behavioral styles as they relate to our personal and professional relationships. The out of balance factor here is a little easier to determine. It is stress. Perhaps it is better said, experiencing significant amounts of stress. Let me emphatically state that style related issues are obviously not the only producers of stress. Some would argue that they may not even be one of the major ones. I'd have to disagree with the last statement, and I'll explain why.

How do personal styles create stress? The answer lies in the relationship between our needs/behaviors and what we actually do. For example, people like myself who are high energy and out-going have a difficult time sitting down to take care of *details*. I can hardly type the word without feeling stressed out. Looking at the piles of paper on my desk and on the floor beside it can really stress me out. I simply don't have time to take care all those details because I am writing this book and working toward a publication deadline.

For Gigi and the others of you who take a more relaxed approach to life, you get stressed out by deadlines, changes in your routine, and living with people like me. You see, when it comes to personal styles and stress, the relationship goes something like this. When you have to work or function for extended periods of time outside your "comfort zone of personal style," your stress level increases.

Since we all aspire to be *style-elastic, mature adults*, we can function in any "zone" required to meet our goals or the needs of others for a period of time. The key is how long we have to do so. It is the extended periods of time that cause the stress. It is not seeing the piles on and around my desk that stresses me out. It is thinking about having to go through those piles *one piece of paper at a time* that does it. (What I really need to do is make an executive decision and get a larger trash can!)

Motivation

The last major subject matter was that of personal empowerment and motivation. You may recall that I discussed personal empowerment in terms of our personal operating systems. It focused on balance of *character, values,* and *personal style operating from a spiritual center.* Personal motivation added the key components of *talents, roles* and *goals.*

Perhaps the "out of balance" condition related to personal moti-vation is the easiest to see. Why? Because you can really *see* this one. People who are unmotivated are usually found going through the motions of life with little energy and drive. If you think this obser-vation is too *style* related, then to see it in the less extroverted people, you need only look as far as the quality of or lack of inter-est in their work. Boredom, lethargy, complaining or total compli-ance are a few of the things that ought to tip us off.

Since the focus here is *personal* and we should know ourselves best, then we should be able to perform the motivation check most easily. To change course (get ourselves re-motivated), we need to re-examine our personal operating systems, the use of our talents, the roles we are playing and our personal goals. We must find opportu-nities to maximize the congruence of these factors. When we are able to do so, the personal motivation level returns propelling us to personal achievement.

How is all this balance stuff related to splitting logs and pulling splinters? I am convinced that *balanced people* spend the necessary time dealing with the logs in their own eyes, leaving little time for pulling splinters out of those of their family, friends and co-work-ers. But lets look for a moment at pulling splinters.

PULLING SPLINTERS

Assuming we have *exorcised* the logs from our own eyes, are we now free to begin pulling splinters or removing specks out of the eyes of others who so desperately need our help? Before we jump into this practice, let me give you the closing words that complete Christ's statement. He said, "You, hypocrite, first take the speck out of your own eye, and then you will see clearly to remove the speck from your brothers."

Starts off pretty strong, doesn't it? Referring to a bunch of people you don't necessarily know as *hypocrites*. We all know what a hypo-crite is. A hypocrite is one who has two sets of rules or standards. The ones they live by, and the ones by which they expect others to live. The word itself is from a Latin word that means *play-acting*. You may recall that in early theater, the actors all wore masks to represent their characters. Hence hypocrites are people who wear masks veiling their true selves or play-acting at character, values, etc.

Once we remove the logs from our own eyes, what happens? He said we would be able to see *clearly*. What does it mean to see clearly? I'd like to suggest three things.

First, having *examined the tools* and given ourselves a "balance" check-up means we are fully aware of our own shortcomings. I have seen that there are areas of my life that need work, help, or improvement. My own humanity has shone clearly. This awareness should be accompanied by increased humility and a much less judgmental spirit.

Secondly, since the logs are removed, I am personally in much less pain. Yet having experienced the pain, I am much better prepared to sympathize with that experienced by someone else. Remember how much getting something in your eye hurts and how debilitating it can be. It usually stops us dead in our tracks. Since I've personally experienced the pain, it is very easy and natural for me to understand and associate with this pain when someone else is experiencing it. The more we understand *seeing clearly*, the more we will be able to *share the pain*.

Third, seeing clearly again allows me to focus on helping others. Now that I have been reminded of my own personal challenges that may require help from others, and experienced pain like others do, I am uniquely qualified to turn my attention to helping others where I am able.

"So, Walter," you ask, "*now* am I able to do some splinter pulling?" The answer is a resounding yes, but . . . When you do, make sure you follow and meet the criteria listed below. It raises exponentially your probability of success in helping others.

1. you have a trust-based relationship with the person you want to help
2. your motive (purpose) is pure: healing not hurting
3. pulling the splinters is actually beneficial to that person
4. it will, at least ultimately, result in a stronger relationship

5. you use a gentle touch, like a cotton swab, not needle-nosed pliers

6. you have the permission of that person (the most important)

Having processed and, hopefully, assimilated the material and information in the book up to this point, you are now ready to move on to the most powerful of the interpersonal tools. Understanding and applying its principles can smooth over the numerous flaws and nicks that occur over time in any relationship. I really do believe that . . .

Only Empowered People Empower Others . . .

This is my favorite (and probably) most powerful keynote address. The reasons are clear to me. It combines what my customers (and I) consider the best elements of any program designed to motivate and equip people to cause change and action. These elements include: passion, the personal side of life as well as the professional, emotion, laughter, and (very importantly) application-oriented content . . . *real stuff, not fluff.*

I say this because as I thought about how I wanted to close this book, I wrestled with what fit best, and what would be remembered. It is said that *we tend to remember what we see or read first and last.* With that in mind, I decided to close the book with this "program." It sounds good on audio tape. I have spots of it on the promo video. Both are well received. But I wondered how it would "feel" written out on paper. So I labored over it to help make it *read* the way it *sounds* because I really do believe that *only empowered people empower others.*

To discuss my thoughts on the concept of empowerment, I like to describe what truly empowered people look like and how they behave using three "E" words. I also like to compare/contrast them with their opposite extreme. People typically fall somewhere in-between the two, but highlighting the two extremes causes people to think about them more keenly.

EQUIPPER OR STRIPPER

The first "E" is *equipper*. The empowerment question is—*Are you an equipper or stripper?* Equippers are those who provide the tools (resources) necessary for others to get the job done. They are suppliers. Their focus is developing *people as our most valuable resource.* Thus they are good stewards of these resources.

Equippers really believe all this empowerment *stuff.* Their actions bear them out. They recognize potential, desire, and talent in others and work to get people the "tools" they need to succeed. They begin at home in the most important relationships. Couples help equip each other. Each partner brings different strengths to the table. These strengths are tools that, when used appropriately and with permission, can help develop or sharpen the other.

One of the primary functions for those of us blessed with children is to equip them. In one of my favorite proverbs, Solomon said *"Train a child in the way he should go, and when he is old he will not depart from it."* There is a lifetime of wisdom in that one. It speaks again to the issues of character, principles, and values discussed previously. When our children leave the nest, are they prepared to face the *real world* with all of its opportunities and challenges?

The counterpart of the equipper is the *stripper.* Ever strip paint off an old piece of furniture? There are two ways I know (there are more I'm sure) that most people use. One is sanding aggressively with sandpaper. The other is using some type of aggressive chemical solution. The first is very abrasive; the second highly caustic.

Some people are like this. Rather than equip or supply what people need to succeed, they strip what they have, leaving behind flesh wounds. When and if these wounds heal, they leave some pretty ugly scars; scars that some people carry with them throughout their lives. Many people carry the scars with them into their various personal and professional relationships.

Ever see the results of strip mining? It is a brutal process. It strips the land of its useful resources and leaves it, for the most part, exposed and bare. People strippers do the same kinds of things. They steal the talent, energy, and other resources that people bring to relationships.

At work, they typically take credit for what other people do or accomplish. They use people as stairs to the top and walk all over them. At home, they use their family to meet their own selfish needs. They steal precious family time to indulge their own hobbies and habits. So I ask you, where do you fall on the continuum line between the equipper and the stripper? I hope you will use these tools to begin building or re-building stripped relationships.

ENCOURAGER OR DISCOURAGER

The second "E" word is *encourager*. The second empowerment question is—*Are you are an encourager or discourager?* Encouragers are true builders. They have a real gift of speaking a timely word. Again Solomon demonstrates his wisdom when he says *"Like apples of gold in settings of silver is a word spoken in right circumstances."* Encouragers find the right word and right circumstances.

One of the great things about encouragement is that it can be learned. It does come a little more naturally to those whose personal styles are more "people-oriented." But it can be learned. And once we learn it, we must use it. For some, it is a *willing* and *able* issue. If I am willing to learn, I can acquire the ability to encourage people, starting with myself.

We all know someone who has this gift. I don't know anyone who doesn't like to be around encouragers. As parents, we try to encourage our young children as they learn new things and master new feats. All of us have applauded their efforts when our little ones began trying to walk. We did it so much so with our last one, that now he runs around the house clapping his hands all the time. Perhaps we went a bit overboard. Not possible! *You can't over-encourage someone.*

When is the last time someone applauded you? When is the last time someone really encouraged your socks off? I bet you remember. You're thinking about it right now. Or perhaps if it hasn't happened in a long time, you're thinking about the encouragers counterpart, the *discourager*.

Discouragers are just the opposite of the encouragers. Instead of building people and relationships, they tear them down. Rudyard

Kipling said "Words are, of course, the most powerful drug used by mankind." He was right. And like drugs, words can remove or inflict pain on people.

We all know these discouragers. If we don't, we see the destruction left behind. It looks much like that left in the aftermath of a tornado. Just a few weeks ago, I was in Memphis working with a client company. My family went with me as my wife is from there, and we lived there seven years during my last corporate tenure. We have many wonderful friends there.

We attended church on Sunday morning and got out about noon. A little over three hours later, much of the church we had just been in was demolished by a tornado. The destruction was swift and great. It will be months before they can return to normal operations. It will be years before they forget what they saw. Perhaps some of the people never will.

So it is with discouragers. Unfortunately, we see their handiwork in the lives of other people. In their children, it shows up as low self-esteem, "I'm no good" kids looking for love and acceptance in all the wrong places (as the song says). It looks like emotionally abused spouses who are torn down and defeated.

At the office, it looks like people, especially managers, who are the consummate fault finders always criticizing what you've done. You just can't please them. The sad truth is they can't please themselves either.

Perhaps we are all need to examine our encourage/discourage ratio. Early in our marriage, Gigi (my wife) and I were talking about *gifts* people have. We may have heard someone give a talk about various types of gifts like encouragement, helping others, giving to others, etc. Anyway, as the conversation continued, I said in a somewhat whimsical tone that I thought I was an encourager. Her retort was "No, you have the gift of discouragement."

Unfortunately, we all know there is usually an element of truth or implied truth in teasing or sarcastic responses. As we continued discussing this, she made another piercing observation. (Regarding her work around the house), she said "You always seem to notice what I didn't get done rather than what I did accomplish." While it was difficult for me to swallow much less accept, it was true. That was early in our marriage and I can (Gigi would) honestly say that it has improved substantially. But I still have to work at it.

It boils down to what, for me, was the essence of Ken Blanchard and Spencer Johnson's excellent work, *The One-Minute Manager*. Try to catch people doing something right, rather than finding what's wrong. And when you do, praise them for it. Pass along an encouraging word. If I had applied that earlier in my own marriage, there would have been less stress caused by my "unconscious discouragement," and my wife would have felt more encouraged by me.

ENABLER OR DISABLER

The third word is *enabler*. An enabler is one who has learned from his own life experiences and is *able* to use what was learned from those experiences to help other people. It is often associated with help in difficult times. In a sense they bring "healing" to others. It may include equipping and encouraging or it could be just propping someone up when they need a brace to lean on.

When we are able to learn from our own difficulties and personal challenges, we earn the rite of passage to become enablers. The most difficult talk I ever had the privilege to write and deliver took place about a year and a half ago. I came home one day from the office, and Gigi said she had just received a call from one of our friends. Chandler was dead. He had accidentally drowned in his family's pool in the backyard. We were stunned. We had just been at their home for a July 4th cookout and pool party the weekend before.

How could something like this happen? Even more difficult to understand was WHY? You see, what made this even more difficult to deal with was that Chandler wasn't my close friend. He was the 3 year old son of my close friend. As any friend does in circumstances like these, you want to help and do anything you can to do so. As it turned out, the way I was best able to help at that time was to be able to speak (share) at the funeral.

I recall afterward, the kind comments about what I shared from the family and others in attendance. People ask how could

I know how to relate or what to share with people after the un-expected death of a little child? The answer lies in learning from life experiences.

It was a day that started off with an early morning date with my extremely pregnant wife, and was to conclude with golf with friends; just a day to remember. We had finally reached the nine month due date with this pregnancy. Gigi and I were so excited. The path to get here had been so difficult. We had been trying to have children for about two years and known nothing but bitter disappointment.

In one year's time we had experienced three early term miscar-riages. Gigi's doctor offered little hope for actually getting and stay-ing pregnant. Staying pregnant was the problem; unlike many whose difficulty is on the conceiving side. Talk about stress in marriage.

Well, with God's grace, some wisdom from a specialist, and a little help from progesterone, Gigi not only became pregnant but carried the baby full term and here we were on THAT day! As I said ear-lier, I took the day off, took Gigi out for breakfast, and then teed it up with a couple of friends. Russ, the head pro at our club is a very good friend and each time I played, I told him to sound the air horn if they called to say that Gigi had gone into labor, and I would come running.

I remember it so well. We were on the 17th hole, and I was ly-ing two as close to the green as I had ever been on that par 5. As we approached the green, Russ came riding up in a cart and told me to get in as Gigi was on her way to the hospital. I remember driv-ing up the wrong side of the road through traffic to get to the hos-pital in record time.

When I got to the labor and delivery room, I found my wife in a hospital bed with people scurrying all around and a fetal monitor strapped across her exposed belly. With tears in her eyes, she looked at me and said "Honey, I'm so sorry, the baby's dead." The monitor showed no heart beat and for reasons unknown to us then, our little girl died the day she was supposed to begin life.

I remember it all like it was yesterday. I will never forget the an-ger, hurt, pain and every other gut-wrenching emotion that we felt.

I think I hurt more for Gigi than myself because of all she had been through; four pregnancies in two years, and all the hormonal and physical things that accompany them. For the next ten to twelve hours, she was in labor giving birth to a child whom the angels had already carried away and gently placed in the "bosom of Abraham." I sat there with her, trying to be an encourager, not knowing what to think, do, or say.

That time in our lives could fill a book in itself. I've already told you about our three kids, God's precious gifts to us. They came during the years that followed. But for Gigi and me, we had learned a few very difficult things through some excruciatingly painful experiences. Over the years, they have helped us *enable* others.

Finally, let's turn our attention to the *disabler*. Most of us have at least some memory of the dreaded disease, polio. It is exciting to know that it was, for the most part, cured and wiped out in our lifetime. But for those who were (and still are) afflicted with it, it was a crippler. We remember the distinctive *polio leg*, typically in a brace of some kind, that was left as a reminder of how crippling it could be. Unfortunately, the disabler is a crippler, too.

Disablers do learn from their experiences. They learn to blame, carry a grudge, or even worse, hate. They carry this baggage with them everywhere they go and make sure that everyone else knows how they got it and who's to blame. Considering themselves the victims, they make others their victims. Disablers aren't capable of forgiving, forgetting or forging ahead.

At home, disablers are masters of creating numerous types of dysfunctional relationships. They may use the techniques of the stripper or the discourager, and they have at least one other one they are very adept at using. They are *reminders*.

Like my company does, I'm sure that many of you have some type of database or time management software on your PC that beeps or makes a noise to remind you of an appointment. When you're in the middle of something else (like writing a book) and deep in thought, these reminders can be real nuisances. They are second only in "obnoxiousness" to the noise you get blasted in your ear when you accidentally call a FAX number! Disablers are like this, except they remind you of what you did, or what the world did to them, and how it has ruined their lives.

At the office, they spend much of their time engaging in *break-room politics* and *departmental* or *(inter-departmental) guerrilla warfare*. They excel in saying that which is expedient or self-promoting and sniping at others. They do whatever they can to make everyone else as miserable as they are. You've heard the expression "misery loves company." They live this out as a *credo* with one slight addition. "Misery loves miserable company."

For extreme disablers, the roots run deep and healing them is very difficult at best. It usually takes a major S.E.E. (significant emotional event) in their lives to open their eyes or some incredibly good counseling/professional help. While most of us don't fall into this extreme category, we still need to examine our own hearts to see what truth there is in what I said above in our own lives.

I've read and heard similar words before, and the message really is true. *It isn't what the trials and difficulties you encounter in life do to you that creates character, but what you do with (or how you respond to) them.* Enablers learn from them, sink the roots of their character a little deeper, and then go about enabling others.

DEFINING EMPOWERMENT

At last I come to the close of this chapter that I hope has caused you to think and look inwardly so that you may serve outwardly. Allow me to close it with my own definition of empowerment. It has three equally important tenets.

Empowerment is giving people the *freedom to win*,
permission to fail, and the *grace to recover*.

Everybody wants to win. There is something within the human spirit that compels us. To a large extent in relationships, whether or not someone perceives themselves a winner depends on your freeing them up to do so.

On the other hand, everybody fails sometimes. This is a given in life. We have all fallen short and missed the mark. Have you given your permission to others to fail, or do they bear the wounds and scars from "friendly fire?"

Finally, once permitted to fail, can we extend to others the grace required to recover? Empowered people do. And I said at the beginning of this chapter, *only empowered people empower others.*

CLOSING

Some Final Thoughts That May Help You Succeed . . .

One of the things that many of us have in common when we come across useful information is trying to figure out how to process and apply it. Whether we just attended a seminar or went through a training program, listened to a tape, or read a book, we often find ourselves overwhelmed with the information. (I've also been underwhelmed, as I'm sure you have. I hope that wasn't the case for you with *Power Tools*.) What do I do with it now that I have it?

The first thing to do is relax. *Think process, not event*. Life is a process, not an event. So are learning and change. This is especially true when it involves people and relationships. My advice is to start with yourself, as we did in the first part of this book. We know by now that we can only really change ourselves. Then you can turn your attention to relationships with others.

The second thing to do is prioritize those things you want to work on changing or improving in order of their importance to you and others. You may want to get input on this from someone close to you (a trust-based relationship). Input from others always brings a reality check for us to make sure we don't go off on some less important tangent.

The third thing to do is to create your own personal development plan. I provided some worksheets in the Appendix to help you get some of your thoughts down on paper as you process them. If you're like me, sometimes we think we have great insight on something and then after not writing it down, we totally lose the thought. It gets suspended in the "twilight zone" of our minds. So learn to write things down.

Fourth, *make* the time to work on and follow up on your plan. Too many strategic plans that organizations develop go no further than their nicely leather bound pages sitting on a shelf somewhere collecting dust. Let's hope the same won't be true for you. But *time* is the most important element.

Fifth, if at all possible, get an accountability partner. This is a person who will help hold you accountable for progress on your plan. It is always helpful to be able to discuss issues, challenges and successes with another person.

Finally, remember one of my favorite adages:

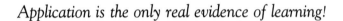

Application is the only real evidence of learning!

So take what you have learned from the principles discussed in this book and apply them in your personal and professional lives. I promise you'll be glad you did. Maybe even more importantly, your family, friends, and the people with whom you work will be as well.

Here to help you succeed in your
personal and professional lives,

Walter

A Tribute

"To those who (over a lifetime) have made and, in some cases, continue to make, an impact on my life through relationships . . ."

Since this book is about people and relationships, I feel compelled to mention those who come to mind, who over my lifetime have helped me along the way. Some of this help was given knowingly, while some came to fruition years later. It is always easier to look back and reflect on what we learned from others. 20/20 hindsight, I guess. Sometimes we are willing students and other times we find we learned from the experiences of our mistakes. Whatever the motive or method, hopefully we do learn and are better equipped to help others as a result.

As it does with most people, my trek starts with my mom and dad who simply did their best for a lifetime to teach us kids "in the way we should go." I really appreciate their love, effort and the impact they have had on my life, *and* the one they are having in the lives of my children. I am also blessed with two loving sisters (Leah and Becky) and their families.

It isn't too often that childhood friends remain that over the long haul. I grew up with two friends who were brothers. Since I had no brothers "by birth," Joey and Duane became my "brothers." We more or less grew up together, and while long distances have separated us for many years, we can pick up where we left off when we do have a chance to talk or visit. Others who were valued friends during these years include Rick, Pick, Graham, Barbara, Rosemary, Art, Raymond, Arch, Jules, Danny, Mike, and Wallene.

College is one of those places you go to learn and have fun; not necessarily in that order! There were some great times and some challenging times during those four undergraduate years at Clemson. One of the first things you learn is about living with someone else . . . roommates. My best one and best friend for those years (who is still a valued friend) was Steve O. You experience a lot together and if you are really fortunate, the bonds that develop during those times are strong enough to hold the friendship intact for decades to come. And ours has done so.

I really appreciate those others who were close during various parts of that experience like Steve V., Steve F., Sally, Ish, Martha Lynn (my cheerleading partner who could even make me look good doing those crazy stunts), and Kathy.

Then there were the *Warsaw days.* Early professional career opportunities often bring incredible learning experiences and solid relationships. I was blessed with both. People like Rick and Becky, Kath, Julie, Heidi and families like the Parkes, Smiths, Renekers, Garrards, Lemons, and Baileys were a real blessing for me during those years.

On the professional side, Dane M. was like a big brother throughout my graduate years and early career years. I really valued his good counsel and friendship along the way. In addition, being a small part of helping birth Biomet was one of the best experiences of my life. It was the people involved who made it so. I really appreciated the "family" we had at that time. Dane and Mary Louise, Niles and Nancy, Ray and Rose, and Jerry and Norma.

During those early career years, two men, in addition to my dad, have been a very strong influence in my life, Gus S. and Phil P. Gus was my first real mentor and friend in every sense of the word; Paul to a young Timothy. I really love this man. Phil is the *friend who sticks closer than a brother,* and we have weathered several storms. I appreciate his continued friendship over the years.

Then it was on to Memphis where life really started . . . marriage and family life that is. The relationships you build during these years have such strong bonds. This was the beginning of many of the best times of my life. God richly blessed me over eleven years ago with a wonderful wife (Gigi). There is no other person in this world I'd rather be with under any circumstances. We, in turn, have been blessed with three incredible children: Trey, Gracie and Zach. I am so proud to be their dad!

I believe those relationships that form out of the experiences of marriage and family are the best and most lasting. During those early years, we established many wonderful relationships with friends we treasure like Mike and Pam, Buzz and Sandra, Steve and Carol, Mike and Janice, Jimmy and Suzie, Russ and Jenny, Bill and Amy, and others. In addition, we have the love and support of Gigi's family.

During those corporate years of professional growth and development, I was privileged to work alongside, and thus befriend, many quality people. Dan H., Jerry M., Bob R., Hank C., Mike K., John P., Steve B., Bruce R., Dennis S., Dom, Debi, Al, Jim W., Jeff, Ken and of course there were numerous others over those years. But the two best friends I ever had that came out of professional relationships are John S. and Bailey L. Together we pontificated solutions to many of the world's problems while consuming bowl after bowl of salsa and cheese dip at lunch. If only the world's leaders would have heeded our "sage advice."

John was also my golfing partner for six years during which neither of us seemed to get any better or significantly lower our handicaps. But we had some fun. Last year, we buried John's wife, and our friend, Charon. It was one of those times that inevitably comes for us all, but too soon in this case. We miss her. We fondly remember, among other things, running around England together and "losing" John in the town of Oxford.

The next phase was a sabbatical of sorts. A career change. A time of soul searching and sorting things out. It landed us in Little Rock. And there we became involved with some of the best and most solid people you could ever hope to know. While the time there was relatively short, I learned much about people, relationships, Gigi and myself during that time. Perhaps we grew and were stretched more during those few years than in any others. We remember and value those people and experiences. Charlie and Karen, Lee and Edye, Bryan O., Mike and Amy, Lloyd S., Linda B., Dave and Pam, Dave and Diana, Steve and Mary, James and Renee, Mike and Victoria, Shack, Dennis and Barbara, Jerry and Cheryl, Robert L. and many other wonderful people committed to that which we all esteem most highly.

Then came the BIG move; starting my own company and relocating. It's Atlanta! Home of the 1996 Olympics. Cold prospecting for business (which to this day I still dislike). The kids start school. Zach is born. *Big,* busy place. Busy people. Difficult to break in personally and professionally. It takes a lot more time than we anticipate. Baseball, soccer, gymnastics . . . we are getting busier by the year. The relationships are fewer than before for many of the reasons listed above. But those we have cultivated, we value. My good friend Crawford. Other good friends like Sterling, John M., Daryl, Eric and Lisa, and my lunch buddy David. Good friends that have come from the professional side like Georgia, Mark, Greg, and Terry. I want to thank Sterling and Nancy for permitting me to share the story about Chandler's funeral.

And finally, a special thanks to those relationships that developed with *real* people in client companies over the years. They are people who are approachable, responsive and value learning themselves. I really appreciate people like them who want to help you do business and succeed. The business world needs more of them.

Enough. It is time to raise my cup and say to all of you, "thank you and God bless you. May you continue to be successful people and build successful relationships throughout the rest of your lives."

POWER TOOLS

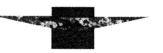

Appendix

APPENDIX

Personal Development Plan

A CHARACTER REVIEW

1. Write down your thoughts regarding the "being" and "doing" sides of character.

Being Side: _____

_____

_____

_____

Doing Side: _____

_____

_____

_____

How balanced are you in both? Which needs more development? Write down a couple of action points you can do to help gain or restore the balance.

1. _____

2. _____

3. _____

2. I listed six attributes that are found in people of outstanding character. Write down your thoughts regarding each. Add to or remove from the list based on your opinions regarding *character*.

Respect: _____

Integrity: _____

Honesty: _____

Moral Absolutes: _____

Responsibility: _____

Courage: _____

3. Write a statement (or two) that defines your character.

_____

_____

_____

_____

PERCEPTION AND PARADIGMS

1. Do you understand the statement "perception is reality" and the context in which it was stated? What does it mean to you?

_____

_____

_____

_____

2. Did you solve the sixteen dot exercise? What does it mean to think "outside the box?" How does it apply to you?

_____

_____

_____

_____

3. Are there any negative paradigms in which you are stuck in your dealings with other people? How can you "shift or un-stick" them? (To best answer this, you will have to think about what was said in the relationships chapters.)

_____

_____

_____

_____

MANAGING EXPECTATIONS

To help you deal with expectation issues, I developed the following chart. Its purpose is to help you get down on paper some of the expectations that cause stress or problems in your life. And hopefully, you will be able to better manage them once you've answered them here. I also included a general example. Yours should be more specific.

Expectation (Problem)	Reality Check (Is it realistic?)	Ownership (Who owns the expectations?)	Control (Who has control over expectations?)	Action Steps to Alter Expectations or Outcome
Trying to please everyone.	Not realistic.	I own them.	They have it.	1. Decide if pleasing people is the "goal." If not, redefine in terms of my goals.

VALUING VALUES

1. From the values clarification grid at the end of Chapter 4, list the five values that you ranked highest.

   1. _____

   2. _____

   3. _____

   4. _____

   5. _____

2. From this list develop a statement of your personal values that incorporates those values that are most important to you from your list above.

   _____

   _____

   _____

3. What people had the most influence on the development of your personal values?

4. Were there any "environmental" areas that had a significant impact on the development of your personal values?

5. What experiences (yours and others) have played a role in the development of your personal values?

6. Do you believe there is a healthy congruence between your character, your personal values and how you live them out? What positive influence does this have on other people? Any negative influence?

PERSONAL STYLE ISSUES

1. What were your primary personal style(s) (represented by the letters—D, I, S, C in Chapter 5)? (You may exhibit more than one. Many of us do.)

D_____I_____S_____C

2. During my discussion of the characteristics (strengths and weaknesses) of each, which one(s) did you relate to most easily and say "does he have me pegged" (as my editor did).

   Strengths

   Weaknesses

3. How can you use this information to improve your ability to help others as well as yourself both personally and professionally?

PERSONAL EMPOWERMENT AND MOTIVATION

1. The "hub of the wheel" when I discussed *personal operating systems* was our *spiritual center*. What is yours? Remember I referred to it as the driving force in your life. What is your driving force? Write it down here.

_____

Now, discuss how it relates to your character, values and personal style. Remember I said it is my belief that they need to be interconnected and congruent. Writing this down will help you think through yours and should help you understand yourself better.

2. What are your talents? What do you do well? Write beside each one an example that sticks out in your mind of how you have demonstrated or used that talent. Finally, are you in a position that allows you to use your talents? Are they developing or deteriorating?

Talent   **Example**

3. What role do you prefer to play? Are you able to function in that role enough to keep you motivated? Are you allowing yourself to be "stretched" in the roles you are currently filling? Write down what you believe would be your ideal job position or role.

4. List your top three goals for this year, personal and professional. Have you laid out plans to accomplish these goals? If not, do so now. What are you going to do to achieve success in reaching your goals?

Personal Goals

1. _____

2. _____

3. _____

Professional Goals

1. _____

2. _____

3. _____

5. On the motivation scale below, where would you rank yourself?

    Low _____ High
           1 2 3 4 5 6 7 8 9 10

Is that where you want to be? If not, what are you going to do to move up the scale?

FORGIVING, FORGETTING, AND FORGING AHEAD

1. As tough as it may be to do, consider making a list of people you need to forgive (or whose forgiveness you need to seek). Now that you've done that, what are you going to do about the list?

2. Similarly, make a list of things you'd like to forget. Do this on a separate piece of paper. When you have finished making your list, fold the piece of paper as many times as you can making it as small as possible. Then throw it away or destroy it, and get on with building success in your life and the lives of those with whom you have the opportunity to do so.

RESPECT, TRUST, INTEGRITY AND COMMITMENT

1. What is the difference as stated in this chapter between *respect* and *trust?*

2. Do you really *value* people? Even those with whom you disagree? How do you demonstrate this?

3. Re-state the T-R-U-S-T acrostic in your own words.

    T—

    R—

    U—

    S —

    T—

4. Can you think of an example where you felt the integrity of a relationship was compromised? It doesn't have to be one in which you were personally involved. What was done, if anything, to restore the relationship?

5. What does relationship *commitment* mean to you? How do you demonstrate it to others in yours?

PERSONAL STYLE ELASTICITY

1. How would you rate yourself on the willing and able scales?

Willing   Low _____ High
              1   2   3   4   5   6   7   8   9   10

Able   Low _____ High
              1   2   3   4   5   6   7   8   9   10

2. What will you do to increase these ratings?

3. Remembering your dominant personal style, which personal style(s) exhibited by others in your relationships seems to create the most problems or stress for you? Do you understand why the problems or stress exist? If so, write it out here. (If not, go back and re-read Chapter 9.)

4. What can and will you do to *flex* your personal style to meet the needs of people like the ones referred to above? Others whose needs and behaviors may differ from your own?

UNDERSTANDING AND INFLUENCE—MOTIVATING OTHERS

1. Interview someone you know (spouse or child) or perhaps someone you work with that appears to have a different personal
   operating system than your own; different spiritual center, values,
   personal style, etc. Conduct this interview with one purpose in
   mind: develop a better *understanding* of that person's personal
   operating system.

2. Next, try to factor in their talents, roles, and personal goals.
   (You may need to do more interviewing to get this information.)
   If it were your responsibility to do so, could you create *influence*
   opportunities to help this person succeed in achieving his or her
   goals?

PULLING SPLINTERS

1. Have you ever tried to help someone get a "splinter" out of his eye with a log sticking out of yours? What was the result? How did the other person respond to you?

2. Have you ever had people offer you "splinter pulling" advice when you didn't want it or didn't feel you needed it? This means they didn't have permission to do so. How did you respond to them or their advice?

3. Describe the conditions that must exist for you to accept "splinter pulling" advice from another person.

4. Keep #3 around with you so that you may refer to it *before* you get the pliers or tweezers out to help someone else pull splinters.

ONLY EMPOWERED PEOPLE EMPOWER OTHERS

1. Write down the names of the most important people in your life.

2. What can and will you do to equip them rather than strip them?

3. When was the last time you spoke a timely encouraging word to those people listed above? If it has been so long that you have to stop and think about it for very long, stop right now, put down this book, and go do so now (or call them right now). Don't wait or put it off for a minute longer.

4. What experiences can you personally draw from that will help you enable instead of disabling those with whom you have personal and professional relationships?

THE SIXTEEN DOT PARADIGM BOX SOLUTION

(There is more than one way to solve this problem.)

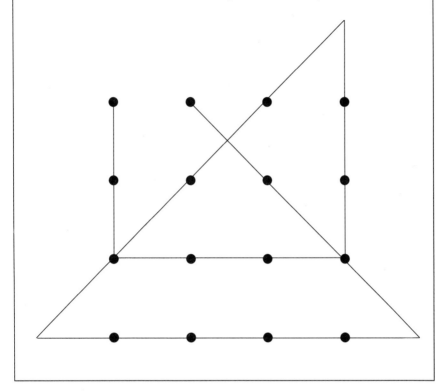

References

Chapter One

Covey, Stephen R. 1989. *The Seven Habits of Highly Effective People*. New York: Simon & Schuster Trade.

Clinton, J. Robert. 1988. *The Making of a Leader: Recognizing the Stages of Leadership Development*. Colorado Springs: NavPress Publishing Group.

Williams, Margery. 1983. *The Velveteen Rabbit*. New York: Alfred A. Knopf, Inc.

Chapter Two

Katz, Robert L. 1956. Human Relations Skills Can Be Sharpened. *Harvard Business Review*, (July): 61.

Chapter Five

Jung, C.G., et al. 1971. *The Collected Works of C.G. Jung, No. 6: Psychological Types*. Eds. Adler, Gerhard, et al. Princeton: Princeton U Press.

Marsden, William Moulton. *The Emotions of Normal People*.

Chapter Seven

Story of adopted girl adapted from the novel *Bits and Pieces*, The Economic Press, Inc., December, 1991.

Chapter Nine

Magee, Robert S. 1985. *Search for Significance*. Texas: Morgan Press.

Chapter Eleven

Covey, Stephen R. 1989. *The Seven Habits of Highly Effective People*. New York: Simon & Schuster Trade.

Chopping wood story adapted from the novel *Bits and Pieces*, The Economic Press, Inc., February, 1992.

Chapter Twelve

Blanchard, Kenneth, and Spencer Johnson. 1982. *The One Minute Manager*. New York: William Morrow & Company, Inc.

A number of the quotations used in this book were taken from *The Columbia Dictionary of Quotations*, Columbia University Press, Inc., New York, 1993 and *Speakers Sourcebook*, compiled by Eleanor Doan, Zondervan Publishing House, Grand Rapids, MI, 1988.

Word definitions as noted were adapted from sources that include: *Webster's New World Thesaurus*, Simon & Schuster, New York, 1985 and *The American Heritage Dictionary of the English Language*, Third Edition, Houghton Mifflin Company, Boston, 1992.

Power Tools©
Programs

PROGRAM TITLES

- *Power Tools for Motivating & Empowering People who Achieve and Succeed*
- *Power Tools for Empowering Organizational Change*
- *Power Tools for Equipping Leaders who Serve*
- *Power Tools for Building High Performance T.E.A.M.S.*

PROGRAM FORMATS

The **Power Tools** programs are available in several formats to provide maximum flexibility for our highly valued clients. These are:

Keynote address (45 min.–90 min.)
Workshop-Concurrent Session (1 hr.–3 hrs.)
Seminar Training program (full day)

BOOKING INFORMATION

To receive a free video promo, references, fee schedule, and program information on how Walter may customize one of the above programs for your organization, please call us at:

(800)-849-6628

Walter Spires

"motivating and equipping people with the tools they need to succeed in their personal and professional lives"

Walter Spires
Product Information & Order Form

Audio Cassette Tapes: (All audio cassette tapes are approximately 30 min. in length.)

From **The L.E.T.S. Do It** Series—This package includes three audio cassette tapes:

Tape #1: L-E-A-D-E-R-S-H-I-P: *The Essentials for Those Privileged to Lead Others*
Tape #2: EMPOWERMENT: *Only Empowered People Empower Others*
Tape #3: SUCCESS with STYLE: *Upgrading Your People Smart Skills*

From the **Empowering Organizational Change** Series:

Tape #1: Change Doesn't Have to Hurt . . . (much)!

Video Tape Program: *Upgrading Your People Smart Skills* (approximately 30 min.)

PRODUCT	PRICE	QUANTITY
Three Tape Package from **The L.E.T.S. Do It** Series	$30.00	_____
Individual Audio Cassette Tapes	$12.00	_____
Video Tape Program: *Upgrading Your People Smart Skills*	$45.00	_____

All prices include taxes and shipping & handling costs.

— —

Please ship the above checked product & quantities to:

Name _____

Company _____ Title _____

Address _____

City _____ State _____ Zip _____ - _____

Telephone Number _____ - _____ - _____

Method of Payment

Check: If paying with personal check, please include home & business telephone numbers and either drivers license or social security numbers. All checks must be received with the order as we do not invoice for materials.

Credit Card ☐ Mastercard ☐ VISA

Credit Card Number _____ Exp. Date _____

Signature _____

Statement of Quality & Customer Satisfaction

We believe that you will be delighted with your product. However if after receiving it, you are not completely satisfied, you may return it to us for a full product price refund. Thank you for allowing us to serve you.

Walter P. Spires, Jr.
President, Designed Excellence, Inc.